STRATEGIC POLICY PLANNING:

A Guide for College and University Administrators

Robert G. Cope
University of Washington

Published by:

The Ireland Educational Corporation
Littleton, Colorado 80122

In memory of
H.J.C.

Published by The Ireland Educational Corporation
2275 East Arapahoe Road, Suite 313
Littleton, Colorado 80122

The publisher acknowledges with gratitude the permission to reprint portions of the work of Thomas Harvey and Douglas Leister first appearing in the Journal of Higher Education.

Library of Congress Catologue Card Number: LC 78-26108
International Standard Book Number: 0-89103-021-2

First Edition

CONTENTS

ABOUT THE AUTHOR

Robert Cope is presently Associate Professor of Higher Education, at the University of Washington. Born in Chicago in 1936, he was educated in the public schools of Chicago and later Michigan where he earned several degrees in business administration and education all from the University of Michigan. He was Director of Institutional Studies at the University of Massachusetts from 1966 until 1969 when he assumed a faculty appointment at the University of Washington specializing in the management problems of colleges and universities. He has held visiting appointments in recent years at the Australian National University and the University of Melbourne and has served as a technology applications consultant for the Weyerhaeuser Company since 1973. He has or is now serving in an editorial capacity with the National Institute of Education, the McGraw-Hill Book Company, the Association for Institutional Research, and the journals Research in Higher Education and Education. His co-authored book on college student retention, Revolving College Doors (Wiley, 1975), is an important resource book for college enrollment maintenance programs. He has also written a substantial number of articles on college management and is an active consultant.

LIST OF ILLUSTRATIONS

LIST OF ILLUSTRATIONS — Continued

FIGURES **PAGE NO.**

Common sense in an uncommon degree
is what the world calls wisdom.
—Samuel Taylor Coleridge

PREFACE

This small volume has only one modest goal: to explain the value of strategic policy planning in a simple, straightforward, common-sense way. I am mindful as I do this of the typical no-nonsense Australian administrator who, after an address at a planning conference in South Australia, said "Planning is merely common sense made incomprehensible by planners!" Embarrassed, I agreed.

Strategic planning is not new or original. I simply expect to open your eyes to what you already do when you systematically make an opportunity analysis. Strategic planning is just that—an opportunity analysis, a way of thinking we all use and understand intuitively. But it is an unconscious way of analysis. I suggest practical ways to go about developing your skills to make the analysis consciously. By ways, I mean approaches for examining the institution's environment, techniques for group creative problem solving, and step-by-step directions for persons assigned the task of leading a planning team.

This book is primarily written for the chief administrative officer whose decisions make policy. It should also be of value to analysts whose data provide the basis for wise policy formulation and to students of higher education. Presidents, analysts, and students should find this open-system, non-regimented approach to planning more useful than the overly-quantitative systems now being tested.

This work offers practical guidelines, not a theoretical exposition. Psychology, sociology, economics, and other disciplines, as well as the less systematic writing of experienced individuals, have provided a considerable body of literature making statements about how organizations do operate or ought to. Such literature has been developing for some time, but I do not consider it developed enough to make more than a modest claim to usefulness.

There have been earlier volumes on planning, on policy formulation, on institutional research, and on academic change, but I believe this is the first book dealing specifically with the promise offered by strategic policy planning, integrating as it does some newer techniques of analysis. The content is intended to help identify undertakings which require long lead times, to help institutions and individuals take initiative rather than merely respond to environmental change, to inspire personal effort as individuals see the value of setting and achieving viable goals, and to help stimulate imagination.

Chapter 1 makes the point that today's colleges and universities don't have a monopoly on instruction and research, since the latter is now shared with independent institutes, hospitals, and large, often multi-national, corporations. Instruction is shared with the military, the media, the business firms (many of which operate their own schools), professional associations, and consulting agencies (witness the airport seminars). In many urban communities there are more classrooms and laboratories on business premises than in schools, and the subjects taught outside the colleges range from the rudiments of communication, through corporate finance, to applied physics. A new educational-management view is appropriate today. Educational, medical, artistic, and commercial functions were known and kept apart too long. Today colleges and universities ought to see themselves as a part of the knowledge industry rather than as a separate institution. It is against this background that college administrators must make analyses, putting opportunity and institutional ability together into more marketable combinations to determine the character of the college or university as it is or is to be.

After the concept of strategy is defined in Chapter 2, I will present techniques that help examine the social and economic environments of the institution, help determine developments and trends in higher education, and help estimate the future opportunity and risks for colleges and universities with varying resources in different settings. An important aspect of the book is the appraisal of the strengths and weaknesses of an institution when viewed in relation to its competition. Thus, Chapter 3 is a study of the environment.

However, since "market" analysis leading to policy is not the whole task, Chapter 4 presents techniques useful for innovative thinking, examples of planning processes, and a ten-step planning process. Chapter 5 provides evaluative criteria. And in Chapter 6 the role of the president as leader for a strategically-planned institution is developed: "the president as architect or strategy".

It is possible to substitute "policy" for "strategy" in much of this discussion; but, as will be made clear later, linking the terms strategy and policy—both virtually undefinable in any practical sense—suits my purpose better. Since policy is one of the major functions, if not the major reponsibility, of those who have to deal with the problems of the total enterprise, the point of view of the president is assumed. Implicit in the presentation is the belief that institutional leadership rests fundamentally on questions of policy; and since the head officer in any organization—whether a business, a government, or a college—must take the responsibility for institutional self-study and for the formulation of goals, this person also plays the major role in establishing the essential character of the institution.

In an era of complexity and increasing specialization, however, it is also important that the specialist possess the ability to recommend and clarify the policy needs of the whole institution; so this book is written for specialists as well—persons who, given the essence of special knowledge, can shape their contributions to the needs of the larger organization. Thus the financial analyst, the chairperson, the counselor, the director of financial aids, the development officer, the assistant dean, and others, to be most effective, must have a sense of the institution's relatively-unique mission, its important strategies. If they don't, they can hardly serve well.

A major point I shall dwell on at length is that institutional policy must be brought into balance with staff (faculty and administrator) needs through informed participation in policy making by those members of the academic community who are capable of looking beyond the narrow limits of their specialties.

There is a large body of literature on policy making for higher education. This literature generally refers, however, to national policy alternatives or to philosophical arguments on the function of universities, the aims of education, the place of science in the curriculum, the compatibility of teaching and research, and the nature of general education. In addition, there are the unsystematically-reported experiences of individuals who have held responsible administrative positions (Barzun, Bennis, Millet), as well as general management concepts taken from psychology, sociology, public affairs, business administration, and economics.

This book takes the position that writings on national policy, philosophy, personal experience, and the outpouring of the disciplines are insufficient. What learned policy analysts, experienced wise men, and our colleagues in other disciplines have to say is often instructive, but the general academic manager, given the particular situation and thus particular problems and opportunities of a unique, post-secondary institution, cannot rely on someone else's experience or on concepts uncritically borrowed from any discipline. Thus, although this book will often allude to the literature, and I shall acknowledge considerable indebtedness to it, for the most part I will use the concept of strategy to provide advice on how to determine and analyze institutional policy.

Dreams put human beings in motion. If the dreams are good enough, they can overcome happenstance and paradox; and the end product will be far more solid than the practical designs of men with no poetry in their souls.

—Norman Cousins, 1977

ACKNOWLEDGMENTS

My first indebtedness is to the selected faculty of the Harvard Graduate School of Business Administration, whose work on business-policy formulation so thoroughly influenced my thinking that I cannot say that there as any truly-original idea in most of the chapters—just my adaptation of their ideas to higher education. I am also indebted to Wayne Gaughran of the Weyerhaeuser Company for sharing literature and challenging ideas; to D. J. Waterhouse of the Australian National University for inspiring the sections on approaches to innovative group processes; to Edward Brodsky-Porges, Judy Gill, Jane Johnson, and Bill Stevens, graduate-student colleagues who critiqued the manuscript over breakfast seminars; and to my colleague Donald Williams, Jr. and publisher Richard Ireland, who both ripped the manuscript to shreds, much to my and the readers' benefit.

Others who perhaps contributed unknowingly include Paul Brinkman, James Doi, Sister Firmin Escher, Stanley Frame, Wendy Gibson, Algo Henderson, George Pierce, Jane Sanders, Thomas Sepic, Claudette, Kathy, and Linda. To so many I owe so much. But I am all they had to work with, so if this small work is not satisfactory, forget them.

Robert G. Cope
Mercer Island, Washington
April 1978

Chapter 1

Wisdom is the ability to see the long-run consequences of current actions, the willingness to sacrifice short-run gains for larger long-run benefits, and the ability to control what is controllable and not to fret over what is not. Therefore the essence of wisdom is concern with the future.

—R. L. Ackoff, 1970

Perfection of means and confusion of ends seem to characterize our age.

—Albert Einstein

THE CONTEXT

The Context of Higher Education in America

The purpose of this brief introductory chapter is to lay out the important contextual dimensions of the American system of higher education as I see it: a surprising diversity of post-secondary institutions, competing in a market economy, using stopgap management techniques on institutions with confused identities, without leadership.

Colleges and universities in North America are not like their counterparts in Britain, the Continent, South America, Australia, or the Communist World in important ways. Varieties of structure, management, sources of support, relation to State and Church, and responsibility to the public make them unique.[1]

In comparison, for example, Europe's post-secondary system is subordinated to State administrations and plans. To be sure, European post-secondary institutions are subject as well to other influences and controls—for instance through organizations for the advancement of research, professional associations, community agencies, student unions,

[1]See for example John Van de Graaff et al., Power in Academia: Evolving Patterns in Seven National Systems, New York: Preager, 1978, in which the particular decision-making structures in seven national systems are summarized in this way:

Federal Republic of Germany .... Politicization and Legalism
France .... Administrative Centralism
Italy .... Patrimonial Politics
Sweden .... Consultative Central Planning
Great Britain .... Autonomy Within a National System
Japan .... State-Sponsored Institutional Hierarchy
USA .... Dispersed Control and Market System

civic groups, and local industries. European institutions also respond to market forces, such as changes in the availability of resources, demands for specific programs, pressures for certain types of research, and so on. Competition for resources, for prestige, and for status, of course, also describes a part of the relationship between European institutions. Yet subordination to and control by a central state administration is the essential feature in all European systems, and, with the possible exception of India, is the essential feature of all other national systems.

In the United States, to the contrary, the market functions more directly as a regulator and a provider of opportunity, since the institutions themselves decide on the admission of students, the hiring of faculty members, the course offerings and requirements, the conclusion of research agreements, the forms of community service, the salary levels, the amount of tuition, and the examination for and awarding of degrees—in other words, all the elements the government officials of at least Continental European institutions have or claim for their jurisdiction. Even the basic elements that institutions share the world over—professors and students—are less homogeneous in the United States, possibily less homogeneous than they were even a few years ago.[2]

Attempts by the Federal Government to intervene (Affirmative Action) or to provide inducements (National Defense Education Act) and even master plans for the further development of public institutions in most of the states have brought about neither central control nor co-ordinated planning. The market and the competitive character of the still highly-independent colleges and universities are expected to continue as the essential regulators of this highly-diversified and overlapping non-system.

To begin with, there are public and private universities, old and new, secular and church-governed, state and municipal, urban and rural. There are four-year colleges content with undergraduate instruction, and others that offer higher degrees in a few subjects. There are even colleges called universities - a title easily conferred during that period of limitless optimism and general excitement. And finally there are junior colleges, community colleges, and vocational-technical institutes.

[2]Even C. Robert Pace's attempt to document the decline of diversity and quality did not demonstrate greater homogeneity. Quite the contrary. See the waffling in Pace's The Demise of Diversity? A Comparative Profile of Eight Types of Institutions (Carnegie Commission technical report, 1974) and J. Victor Baldridge et al., "Diversity in Higher Education: Professional Autonomy", Journal of Higher Education, 48:4, July-August 1977, 367-388.

Michigan's Colleges and Universities

The state of Michigan illustrates how even the public sector cannot be viewed as a monolith. The University of Michigan at Ann Arbor, of course, continues to be the pre-eminent intellectual model, with liberal and cultural overtones—a hybrid between the prestigious private university and the public land-grant university. Michigan State University at East Lansing, while one of the academic success stories of recent decades, still lacks the intellectual and social prominence of the University of Michigan. Michigan State is the megapopulist university: agricultural, vocational, and applied. Wayne State University, in mid-Detroit, is distinctly urban and commuter. Former regional teachers' colleges (Northern, Central, Eastern, and Western), only universities in name, still emphasize teacher training and serve the lower-middle-income class.

Michigan Technological University and Ferris State College, emphasizing applied technology and engineering, are providing still other alternatives. One of public higher education's newest developments is found in every region and every large city: the community-junior college. Like the comprehensive high schools on which they have been modeled, community-junior colleges serve the student going on to a four-year college; the student who only wants a two-year terminal, general education program; and the student who needs a vocational or semi-professional skill.

Michigan's less-than-monolithic public sector also has Oakland University, which is now more like a typical public college of arts and sciences, but retains some of its original highbrow-academic-intellectual culture. There is also Grand Valley State College, the newest public, liberal-arts college. And there was Monteith College, Wayne State University's experiment in general education with a social-science/humanities orientation in a community atmosphere.

Michigan's private sector, while not having as much diversity or as many institutions as other states east of the Mississippi, has substantial variety: Aquinas, Calvin, Mercy, and Nazareth Colleges suggest the diversity of religious orientations. Soumi and Hope Colleges, which also have church ties, serve the Finnish and Dutch. Among other Michigan private colleges, Siena Heights is widely recognized for its art and literature, Albion for science, Marygrove for art, Madonna for serving adult needs. Kalamazoo emulates the recognized Eastern liberal-arts colleges. Alma, Andrews, Concordia, Cranbrook, De Lima, Duns Scotus, the Detroit Institute of Technology, the General Motors Institute, Glen Oaks, Hillsdale,

Lawrence, Madonna, Northwood, Olivet, Spring Arbor, and the University of Detroit, each distinctive in its own way, round out the spectrum of public and private options in one state.

Most private colleges are invisible nationally; however within the locale, faith, or economic group each institution customarily serves, it is well known and is no less visible than local public colleges. Consider Grand Rapids: Like most medium-size cities, it has a low national profile, as have its substantial number of post-secondary institutions. In addition to Aquinas College (liberal-arts and Dominican), the Grand Rapids metropolitan area has Calvin College (liberal-arts and Christian Reformed Church), Grand Rapids Junior College (third-oldest in the United States), Grand Valley State College (public, liberal-arts), Davenport College (a business college on the verge of regional accreditation) and Kendall (a well-regarded school of design). Three of the state's major public universities also offer degree-credit extension in Grand Rapids.

The point of going into detail for Michigan and Grand Rapids is to emphasize the diversity, availability and otherwise national invisibility of the nevertheless active and competing post-secondary system. Even greater variety in academic environments ("product options for the consumer) occurs in most other states, especially among the most distinctive liberal-arts colleges: expressive Bennington, intellectual Swarthmore, vocational Rensselaer, protective St. Mary's, collegiate Miami (of Florida), and the experimental colleges: Goddard, Antioch, Reed. The prestigious private universities, the colleges of Black Americans, the academies for the Armed Services, the new experimental public colleges, the residential colleges within the multiversity, the urban colleges, the open universities, the colleges for ethnic groups, and a substantial proprietary sector all add to the diversity and to the complexity of management, especially when resources tighten and competition heightens among institutions for students, federal funds, athletes, and research projects, and heightens at the same time with other organizations having educational interests (such as the YMCA) and with other public goods and services.

Common Difficulties Throughout the System

Clark Kerr and Earl Chiet have noted that colleges and universities suffer and can be expected to suffer for a long time from common difficulties. They spend huge sums, yet are desperately poor; their faculties are restless; their students assail them; their neighbors distrust them. The public they serve is critical of rising tuitions, unsatisfactory admissions policies, and ever larger classes, yet the public keeps making more and more demands for turning out scientists and engineers; for training retail clerks and computer programmers; for providing cultural and sports entertainment; for satisfying diverse values in morals, in the arts, in politics; for curing illness; for improving seeds; for fostering international understanding; for aiding the less privileged; for building useful job skills while preparing persons for leisure and culture.

The new functions colleges have taken on and the methods improvised during the recent two decades of expansion and seeming limitless answering, coupled with continued confusion about what higher education is, have badly distorted, if not torn, the academic robe of the formerly single-purpose and easily-defined institution. Since we have placed our institutions at the call of many publics, often unknown to one another and frequently contradictory in their demands, it is not surprising that our publics, our clients, our supporters are bewildered. Unfortunately, our institutions are little better understood by those within. Witness the seemingly endless "guerrilla warfare"—part organized, part fortuitous. The internal stresses, if they do not emerge as votes of no confidence, sit-ins, or organized union resistance, at least emerge as enervating campus gossip: "Why is this being done? Is it the president, or perhaps the trustees?" "Why aren't we doing that? Didn't the administration listen? Doesn't the administration understand?" "Why weren't we consulted? After all, it is part of our responsibility, isn't it?" "Why weren't we told? It is our college; after all, we are the institution (faculty)."

The public, the legislature, and the trustees, faculty members, students, and administrators in many institutions suffer from lost comprehension. Having lost an informed view of what the institution is or is to be has now brought about the introduction of a myriad of new stopgap management techniques, aimed at clarifying for the short term what we are about: program budgeting, management by objective, management information systems, offices of institutional research, planning offices, behavioral objectives, performance accountability, national centers for higher-education management study, and multitudinous other "mechanical" excesses using inputs, outputs, MBO, RPM, PEFM, weighted credit hous and unit costs to move us toward thinking we are regaining a measure of control. In fact, we are simply getting more reams of computer output.[3] It is an activity trap.

[3]See Stephen Dresch, "A Critique of Planning Models for Post-secondary Education", Journal of Higher Education, May-June 1975, 245-286.

A central thesis of this book is that this patchwork of devices will lead to further paralysis rather than action, to futility rather than utility, to bankruptcy rather than solvency. The patchwork leaves academic managers searching for synthesis, and confused. The managerial revolution forecast by Rourke and Brooks (1966) brought about the triumph of technique over purpose,[4] and as such leaves one hungering for synthesis and for leadership.

> *Good management has always been beneficial to colleges; the difference today is that it is becoming easier to recognize the symptoms of bad management.*
>
> —*Fred Harcleroad, 1970*

[4]"Triumph of Technique Over Purpose", Wallace Sayre's phrase.

Chapter 2

> *It may be different in your college or university, but in the institutions that I know the planning process usually has all the serenity and thoughtful rationality shown by that hypothetical man who was hip-deep in alligators, when someone ordered him to drain the pond.*
> —*Franklin Patterson, 1977*

> *In the nature of things, greatness and unity go together; excellence implies a center.*
> —*John Henry Newman*

THE CONCEPT OF STRATEGY

It is the purpose of this chapter to develop the idea of strategy, clarify the uses and limitations of the concept, and identify some problems policymakers may expect to encounter in choosing between strategic alternatives.

Before discussing the parameters of strategic planning, however, I wish to take a brief excursion into an arena where pedagogical nonsense has been diverting our attention to a non-issue too long. When employing recent concepts of management, especially when applying the concept of strategic planning, it is not necessary to attempt to differentiate between policy makers and administrators or between policy making and decision making.

Strategic planning as a management function cannot be properly understood or discharged with unnecessary differentiations as to who or what constitutes "administration" or "management". Confusion is further enhanced in the university, where everyone wants to participate in "governance". It serves my purpose just as well to take what may appear to be mild liberties with the language by using decision making as though it were synonymous with managing, which in turn is synonymous with planning and governance.

In each instance I refer to the collective exercise of foresight; and since foresight is required in all decisions, planning becomes in practice identical with decision making on the part of those with management or policy-making responsibilities. Now those members of the institution's staff who facilitate the determination of what is to be done I take to be policy makers; while those members of the staff who facilitate the co-ordination of whatever it has been determined to do I take to be administrators. And since in modern management practice individuals perform both roles, there is no point in differentiating between policy makers, managers, and administrators, just as there is no point in differentiating between the acts of policy making, planning, and decision making. Everything is clear as long as the college, university, or department knows what it is doing. The worst problems that administrators, trustees, faculty members, and planners get themselves into—misunderstandings, confusion, votes of no confidence, firings, and internecine warfare—are the result of spending too much time trying to decide on who decides what. Purpose attracts commitment. Purpose gets co-operation. Effective leadership today encourages participation without regard to the non-issues of place in the organization. Leadership is effective when it clarifies quality of purpose through strategic planning. If institutions know what strategy they are following, they know what they are doing. And if they know what they are doing, who decides what isn't important. The prescription is simple: The institution's strategy must dominate questions of structure and process. The principal criterion for all decisions should be relevance to the achievement of purpose through a strategy unique to each institution.[1]

Strategy Defined

The term "strategy" emerged from military usage. The meaning suggests the deployment of armed forces so as to meet an enemy in combat under advantageous conditions. The term also carries the unfortunate connotation of trickery or deception in the minds of many. In recent years, however, the term has taken on a more positive image as it is used to describe the "strategy for research on cancer" or the "war on poverty" or a strategy to deploy national resources to aid the economy. There is a "strategy for peace", a fund-raising strategy, a vote-getting strategy, a marketing strategy, and an energy-conserving strategy.

The intended meaning of strategy is extended here to encompass an institution's choice of goals, the plans for achieving these goals, and the deployment of resources to attain these goals. Strategy is the pattern of objectives, purposes, or goals and major policies and plans for achieving these goals stated in such a way as to define what the college or university is or is to become. Strategic policy planning results in: (1) the determination

---

[1]For a "serious" discussion of these differences (if they are differences) see Herbert A. Simon, "The Executive as Decision Maker", The New Science of Management Decision, New York: Harper and Row, 1960, 1-8; Geoffrey Lockwood, "Planning in a University", Higher Education, 1:4, 1972, 409-434; R. L. Ackoff, A Concept of Corporate Planning, Wiley-Interscience, 1970, particularly Chapter 1; Robert G. Schroeder, Management Information Systems for Colleges and Universities, Working Paper Series, Management Information Systems Research Center, University of Minnesota, 1975; or Jon F. Wergin, "The Evaluation of Organizational Policy Making: A Political Model", Review of Educational Research, 46:1, Winter 1976, 75-115.

of the basic long-range goals of the institution, and (2) the adoption of courses of action and (3) the allocation of resources necessary for reaching these goals—all being integrated and unseparable.

John Millett's (1974) statement on what he calls policy planning captures most of the concept:

> I am disposed to think of policy planning as the resolution of the major issues entailing value judgments, major issues of social goals, and the proper means for achieving the desired goals. Policy planning is also concerned with how to obtain the economic resources with which to pursue desired goals, and the setting of priorities among goals. (Page 57)

Marvin Peterson (1971) makes approximately the same point: "Policy decisions, the broadest and most encompassing decisions, are those concerned with a college's or university's long-term objective, its program goals and strategies for achieving them, and its strategies for obtaining the necessary resources." (Page 27)

I would only add here that my concept of strategic planning places more emphasis in an economic sense on the position of resources—fiscal, human, physical, and intellectual—so as to maximize opportunities in the institution's environment: Strategic planning is opportunity analysis. Strategic policy decisions are, for example, those concerning:

1. Choosing mission, goals, and objectives
2. Deciding on organizational structure
3. Acquisition of major facilities
4. Starting new majors/degrees or dropping existing majors/degrees
5. Establishing policies or strategies relating to academic programs, support services, personnel, facilities, and financing
6. Gross resource allocation (budgeting) to organizational units and programs

The results of strategic planning set the direction for the institution. For example, most institutions classify as "planning" activities such as scheduling classes; assigning faculty members to classes; scheduling rooms; controlling student registration; implementing admissions rules; scheduling and assigning staff members; formulating and controlling detailed budgets; planning and controlling personnel levels; determining curriculum changes; hiring faculty and staff members; and measuring, appraising, and improving personnel performance. The proper term for activities such as these is "operations management" or "operational control".

Strategic planning is concerned with the long-term development of the institution, its essential character, its personality, its essence. Therefore, strategic planning is concerned with decisions which have enduring effects that are difficult to reverse.

Bennington, Reed, Michigan, Chapman, Texas A and M, Chicago, Lesley, Mount St. Mary's, Cleveland State, and other—especially the well-established—colleges and universities have "personalities" which more or less clearly reflect aspects of intent that are manifested in initial appointments, in tenure decisions, in the recruitment of students, in the selection of new course offerings, in the development of public service, and in the choice of new presidents. The central character of an institution as established as Yale, for example, is likely to be unchanged even though there are substantial changes in the allocation of resources internally (closing its education department in the late 1950s), or admissions arrangements (going coeducational, adopting the contingent-loan program), or architecture (erecting the Tootsie Roll Tower), or personnel policies (implementing the Affirmative Action Plan), or the myriad of other areas in which changes made year-by-year reflecting the gradual evolution of the socio-economic environment and day-to-day responses by Yale to problems and opportunities.

For both the clearly-established and less well-established institutions, I wish to demonstrate the need for strategic thinking that captures the present special and distinctive competencies of institutions, and projects that character into the foreseeable future. I am indifferent to the test of a firm definition and further refinement (or defense) of a particular meaning for the key concept as long as I can clarify the usefulness of the concept by illustration and application. Perhaps the ambiguity of meaning is desirable. The reader is urged to develop the concept presented here in ways which are personally useful, given each person's and each institution's particular situation.

Strategy Formulation and Implementation

Strategy has two equally-important aspects: formulation and implementation. The formulation of strategy is a planning activity consisting of several clearly-interrelated sub-activities including: (1) identification of opportunities and problems in the institution's environment and estimation of the degree of opportunity or degree of risk associated with discernible alternative decisions; (2) assessment of the institution's strengths and weaknesses; (3) consideration of the personal values, aspirations, and ideals of staff members, donors, and publics; and

(4) contemplation of the institution's responsibility to the public. In brief, an assessment of the might do and should do.

The ability to determine these four components of strategy, while difficult to develop, is easy compared to the art of reconciling their possibly-divergent implications. For example, the new president of a church-related college in the Southwest with declining enrollments and income may see that employment-related instruction at local military installations is a way to enhance enrollments and income, especially since other competing institutions in the region are not serving this market. The faculty and the administrative staff are experienced, however, only in providing a traditional, church-related, liberal-arts program for students just out of high school. The president, staff and trustees, in addition, may believe that vocational courses deter learners from obtaining wisdom which can be acquired only through the study of the intellectual disciplines in a Christian setting. They all recognize, however, that the mission of the church is to share its resources for the benefit of all mankind, and the charter granted by the state contains provisions to conduct the college's affairs in the public interest. Furthermore, the president knows that the continuance of military installations in that area is in some doubt; there is talk within the denomination about merger with a similar denomination having a college which might be merged as well; and the Director of Admissions now has data showing that early admissions for next year's freshman class (for that time of year) are at an all-time high.

Obviously, before a unified strategy can be achieved in this institution something will have to give: The present status is not tenable for long; the market opportunity is tentative; the competence and resources of the college are one-dimensional; the institution's traditions and values give mixed indications of which way to turn; and the strategy must be adaptable to changes both in the denomination and in the environment. Almost every college and university faces dilemmas equivalent to these. The techniques of strategic policy formulation presented in Chapters 3 through 5 are intended to alleviate—not eradicate—predicaments of this magnitude.

For fear that what I advocate in the way of strategic positioning will be read simply as opportunism, especially by those from the distinctive private colleges (distinctive implying different, not necessarily elitist), allow me to assure the reader that I do not advocate strategic policy planning simply to increase applicant pools, attract donors, or ease financial stress, without concern for how changes affect campus educational and cultural environments. I am concerned about maintaining the distinctive ambience that is theirs so that the effect they can have on higher education generally will be preserved. Bowen and Minter (1975) put it well:

> One major question. . . .is of whether, in the struggle for survival, the basic integrity of private colleges and universities is threatened. With the growing intensity of competition for students and funds, are they being forced to respond to market forces in ways that impair their distinctiveness, their academic excellence, their concern for human scale and individual personality, their commitment to liberal learning, their role as a sanctuary of academic freedom, their position as standard-setters? It would be a hollow victory if the private sector were to survive and even prosper financially at the expense of giving up the characteristics that make their survival important. (Page 79)

Other readers of this work may assume that strategic policy planning is merely a "front" for "marketing", with marketing's connotation of "Madison Avenue"-style huckstering. David Trivett (1978) offers the view I believe most appropriate today:

> In application to the administration of higher education, marketing is an approach or "philosophy" of management and planning based on the conviction that those institutions that survive respond to basic needs felt by its members of the population the organization seeks to interact with, its markets. Markets are the subgroups of the publics an institution has....College and university administrators who employ marketing concepts recognize that the survival of an institution depends on the identification and fulfillment of the needs of their chosen clientele in a manner consistent with the educational purpose of the institution. (Pages 2-3)

The Functions of Strategy

Colleges and universities do plan strategies unconsciously. Conscious attention to strategy is necessary, however, to give mission statements operational substance. Mission statements are strategic policy statements. They abound with phrases about developing ideals, breadth of view, adding to the general culture, providing for the fullest development, maximum enrichment, richest celebration of life, and so on. Mission statements are essential; they provide a flavor, a model, an inspiration that no college or university can be without. But they are not completely adequate, because they do not say how their noble ideals are to be accomplished. What is the pattern of objectives, purposes, or goals and major policies, and what are the plans for achieving them?

An important objective of strategic policy formulation is to go beyond typical mission statements to set visible goals. Visible goals serve to focus personnel effort and can increase personal motivation; individuals can see how their needs and responsibilities fit the direction in which the institution is moving and thus are less likely to be administering policy or moving in a direction that is inconsistent with the carefully-arrived-at emphases of the institution. Most of us have been in organizations or even smaller professional groups (such as departments or committees) in which we understood the mission, but knowingly—or worse, unknowingly—did not seek action that was consistent with the usually unstated (implied) goals.

Although the utility of setting visible goals may considerably aid individuals, by showing them how their actions harmonize with the institution's strategy, a more important function is to provide a basis for affecting and changing future developments which might otherwise endanger the institution's program. Many universities, when anticipating the long-range planning report (the Master Plan) of newly-established state co-ordinating councils, have produced (often for the first time in decades) a plan that seeks to preserve their domain in such terms as "We are this way, and we want to stay that way." Since this type of plan seldom meets more than a few of the criteria for the evaluation of a strategic plan spelled out in Chapter 5, it is insufficient except as a stopgap defensive maneuver. Most institutions—nearly 100% unfortunately—rely on favorable circumstances and currents—sometimes colorful intuitive leadership. This is simply adaptation to circumstances. Reliance on adaptation and intuitive leadership (occasionally from the faculty) leaves the institution at the mercy of the strongest currents. Innovation and creative strategic planning, on the other hand, enable an institution or individual to carve out a future rather than simply respond to favorable and unfavorable currents.

Political, economic, social, technical change are a part of the environment, as is intense competition among institutions for students, grants, donors, favorable legislation, faculty and staff members. Adaptation and its short-term relative improvisation, however creative or even brilliant, are insufficient as management techniques today because of the negative effects of the turbulent environment and the heightened competition. The range of alternative responses planned well in advance and incorporated into strategic plans are generally wider and wiser than decisions made on the spur of the moment. Most programs, because they take long development and hundreds of thousands if not millions of dollars, must necessarily be considered in detail and in relation to the total institutional program well in advance. The time has passed when new moves can be made without comprehensive advance planning.

The Limitations of Strategy

The practice of strategic planning is not without limitation. It will not erase the inevitable conflict between institutional and departmental goals or between institutional and departmental and personal goals. The arts faculty will still have to repel the advances of the barbarians from behind the ramparts of high culture; the dean of the faculty will still be the dean of the administration; parking will still be the one cause uniting the academic community in mortal combat; and to avoid ugly and noisy clashes there will still be hidden agendas to conceal the what's-best-for-me game plan. These are manifestations of the competitive propensities among academic tribes, and are preferable to sloth and stagnation. Even strategic plans arrived at through informed participation by the entire academic community and articulated persuasively by the administration and faculty leadership will never have the same meaning or appeal to all parts of the institution or to all individuals within it; but I maintain that the likelihood of undue competition that can bring institutional decision making to a grinding halt is greatly reduced with strategic policy planning.

Another serious limitation is that strategic long-term planning, given increasing complexity and an accelerating rate of change, becomes more and more difficult. It is impossible quantitatively to predict the future in detail, and thus complete accuracy in forecasting is not possible. It is particularly difficult to chart the posture of Federal involvement in post-secondary financing, the legislation and administrative regulations in fifty different states, and court decisions at both the state and the federal level. However in today's turbulent, changing, and competitive world it becomes even more important to look searchingly into the future and study a variety of alternatives in advance, so that the possibility of surprise is reduced and plans can be prepared for a wide range of possibilities. The more uncertain the future, the more essential it is to contemplate what is likely to happen and to assign probabilities to the recognizable possibilities. Predicting public policy in particular is becoming more necessary for sound planning, and I will have more to say about this in Chapter 3.

An even more serious limitation is that an institution may become so committed to a plan that an unanticipated opportunity is not considered. For example, it may be impossible to know in advance what discoveries in research will bring forth in new sources of funds for research universities, what a new environmental crisis will mean for the re-education of adults by community colleges, what a new life-style will mean for continuing education, what a new technology will mean for instruction, or what a wealthy donor may offer a small liberal-arts college. Perhaps simply maintaining a position (a strategy) of complete flexibility to take advantage of unanticipated opportunity is more important than commitment to a long-term plan. Obviously the determination of strategy cannot be so solidified that it cannot accommodate uncertainties (threats as well as opportunities). Strategy formulated by balancing commitment and flexibility, evolving in the direction of improving the relationship between the institution and its environment, should be the most difficult task facing chief executives in colleges and universities today and tomorrow.

This concept of strategy is not a substitute for judgment; it is the principal aid to judgment. The greatest limitation is not inherent in the concept itself, but lies in the difficulty of conceiving a realistic pattern of goals that is optimal for a given institution. How to begin is the subject of the next chapter.

No college or university, private or public, now has or can hope to have the resources needed to do everything well. An institution will have to decide whether to do a few things well or many things poorly.

—Fred Harcleroad, 1970

Chapter 3

I'm afraid of the dark and suspicious of the light.

—Woody Allen

We are confronted with insurmountable opportunities.

—Pogo (Walt Kelly)

ANALYSIS OF THE ENVIRONMENT

The inexactness of the concept of strategy and the limitations to the usefulness of this concept in practice, especially in the face of a changing environment have been stressed. Strategic planning is an art, evolving its own processes. Although an art with all the nuances of an art, I take the position that an institution guided by a clear sense of purpose with strategic plans rationally arrived at and openly committed to, is likely to be more vital and thus serve the social good better than an institution whose future is left to improvisation.

Determining a workable pattern of goals and objectives and processes for achieving them starts with identifying the opportunities and risks in the institution's environment. Here we shall examine some of the complexity and variety in environmental forces.

First, it must be observed that the environment of an institution, as of any living entity, is that pattern of all the external conditions (social, political, economic, technological) that influence the institution's life.

A part of the planning "model" for scanning the environment can be represented by the four-sided framework illustrated in Figure A. The primary dimensions are economic, social, political, and technological. Foreseeing what will happen or even recognizing what is already happening in the total environment of an institution may present one with the feeling of facing a problem of staggering proportions. There are techniques, however, for gathering and organizing intelligence about the changing nature of those forces vitally affecting higher education generally and your institution in particular.

Socio-political-economic-technological forecasting is one such technique. Like strategic planning, forecasting too is an art. It is a skillful art in application.

First, it is necessary to continuously and comprehensively monitor the environment. Probably the best example of this continuous monitoring is in the insurance industry under the leadership of the Institute of Life Insurance, which has instituted a Trend Analysis Program (TAP) based on a matrix integrating publications on one axis and the other segments of the environment (politics, population, social change) on the other. Individual insurance companies are assigned to monitor different cells of the matrix for evidence of trends in that segment of the environment. The monitoring companies report regularly, and the Institute synthesizes their observations.

For particular colleges and universities, a simplified way of scanning the "public policy" environment is to assign the responsibility to the Office of Institutional Research or to an Office of Planning. Since public policy tends to change slowly and grows through the accumulation of individual events (Kibbee, 1973), one might begin by simply following carefully the new ideas that appear in the literature of higher education, and keeping track of those that seem to develop a following. Reports of some of the larger and thus more influential foundations (Carnegie, Exxon, Ford) should be examined for their ideas and concerns. Likewise, there are certain elected governmental officials, agency heads, and opinion leaders whose public statements provide useful information when certain ideas reoccur with increasing frequency. Certain states tend to be harbingers of educational change and thus their public policy decisions, either in the legislatures or in the courts, should be monitored. Of course court decisions, particularly in the Supreme Court, need to be examined closely. The Chronicle of Higher Education, The Futurist, Change, the London Times Higher Education Supplement, editorials, and the like, along with major addresses at national conferences, are among important sources of "futures" information.

Education Administration Abstracts uses the following alphabetically-arranged categories for summarizing societal factors influencing education, and I find their list sufficiently comprehensive:

Automation, Science, Technology
Church-State Relations
Human Resources
Economic Development
Governmental Relations
International Relations
Minority-Group Relations
Urban and Metropolitan Affairs

Figure A

CONCEPTUAL REPRESENTATION OF ENVIRONMENTAL CROSS IMPACTS

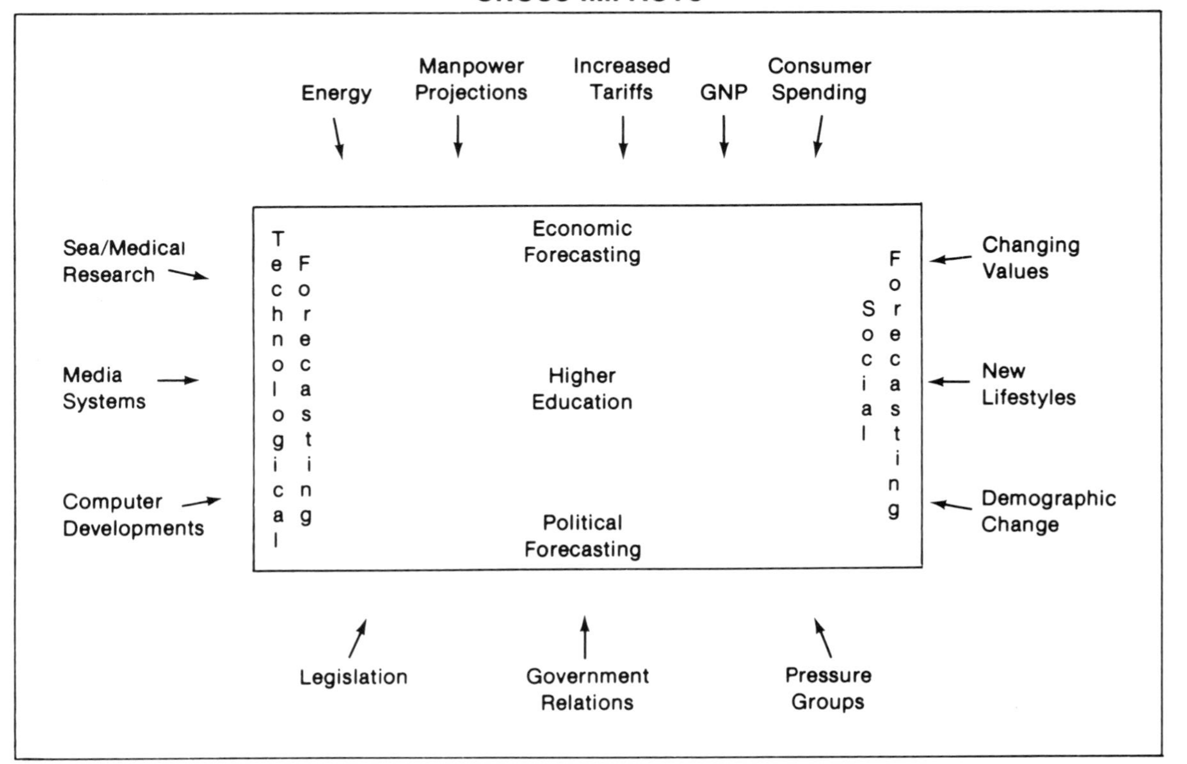

Population Changes
Social-Class Structure and Mobility
Values

However the monitoring is done, it must be translated into patterns having particular application to individual institutions. Hundreds of separate items of information suggesting trends will only saturate the planning system. So it is necessary to see patterns in the trends—patterns which enable us to see the significance of isolated events and to analyze the cross-impacts of one trend on others so management will have an improved understanding of the probable course of events. For example, Harvey (1974) suggested that contrary to indications in the early 1970s and even at this writing (1978), "we will in all probability see decreased emphasis on undergraduate vocational education over the next 25 years". He sees a pattern emerging from these seven observations:

1. Well over 50% of all students graduating from college enter professions for which they receive no professional preparation.

2. Achievement in college, as measured by grades, bears little significant relationship to achievement in post-academic situations. Factors such as motivation, socio-economic background, and self-concept bear much stronger relationships to success.

3. Knowledge is expanding at such a geometric rate that it is becoming increasingly difficult to master even a significant minority of extant knowledge in any given field.

4. College graduates are finding that the knowledge they acquired as undergraduates quickly becomes obsolete.

5. Related to all of these factors is the current crunch in the labor market and the increasing disregard of many young people for material accumulation.

6. It is becoming increasingly clear that, for the future, non-vocational efforts will become more time-consuming than employment. The National Association of Business Economists projects some interesting statistics. Hypothetically, let us assume that you all work a 40-hour week and begin employment at age 21. According to the NABE you will retire at age 38, after essentially only 17 years of vocational life.

7. Professional and vocational certification is beginning to be separated from collegiate preparation. Nursing, law, medicine are all devising alternate certification mechanisms. The real question mark, though, rests with the Supreme Court. In Griggs Versus Duke Power Company (1971), 91 Supreme Court 849, the Supreme Court unanimously ruled that a job could

> not be denied on the basis of non-receipt of a high-school diploma where such non-receipt could not be shown to disqualify competence. The extension of this case could well be significant. If the BA were no longer a necessary access credential to many jobs, such as salesman, how many students would abandon traditional higher education for alternative institutions? (Pages 518-519)

The point, once again, is to illustrate how facts, research data, court decisions, and trends taken from many sources must be synthesized as Harvey has done. Patterns must be identified. The same pattern may then have quite different effects on institutions with different "profiles" in different communities in the same locale. A swing away from the vocational would have quite different effects on Union College and Rensselaer, and no effect at all on Vassar.

There are no islands any more.
—Edna St. Vincent Millay

Tools and Techniques for Forecasting

Forecasting changes in the environment is hardly an exact science; it is the application of intelligence to information. That information, however, is subject to more systematic gathering, as already suggested, and is amenable to other forms of display. In addition to the relatively well-known and, in some applications, sophisticated techniques already developed for trend forecasting, Delphi forecasting, scenarios, and "cross-impact" analysis, I offer for consideration two tools that may be of some additional value, with an all-too-acute awareness of their limitations and lack of sophistication.

1. The Probability-Diffusion Matrix

In predicting developments over decades, it is meaningful to think of degrees of relative probability rather than of certainty or inevitability; for in the final analysis the assignment of a probability to a trend or future pattern of related events is a matter of judgment, but one based on weighing known data and cross-checking with expert opinion. Part of that expert opinion can be supplied by your faculty members. Get them involved.

Cross-checking can be made more exacting by developing a probability-diffusion matrix, as illustrated in Figure B, in which predictions are stated along a probability axis so that their relative positions can be made apparent.

Figure B

PROBABILITY/DIFFUSION MATRIX FOR EVENTS AND TRENDS OCCURRING IN THE UNITED STATES AND WORLD BY 1990

Probability: Low → High (columns); Diffusion: High → Low (rows)

Low				Probability				High
Thermo-nuclear war						8 +% inflation		
					30-hr. work week		Minerals extracted from oceans	Rising levels of education
			Sky-trains across both oceans			Energy crises	Less traditional higher educ.	
					Third World relatively poorer			
				Retirement at 55			Multi-national unions	3.5-5% unem-ployment
	Urban riots		Ecological crises			More business-government partnerships		
		Strikes outlawed			Fresh water crises		Localized solar heaters	$4,500 per capita income
						Regional conflicts		

*Adapted from Ian H. Wilson, "Socio-Political Forecasting: A New Dimension to Strategic Planning," Michigan Business Review, July 1974, p. 15-25.

It is also useful to assess the probable diffusion of a trend or pattern of events as it affects different populations the college serves. The same trends may have different impacts or no impact on different segments of the population. Again, by plotting predictions along a diffusion axis one makes explicit in a more co-ordinated fashion the probability of trends, of possible futures.

When these two axes are combined as shown in Figure B, a greater appreciation for interactive effects and internal consistency should be achieved. I hasten to add that the plottings made in this matrix are for purposes of illustration only, are not sufficiently thought out, and thus are offered only to incite the planners' interest in this technique. Other versions of cross-impact matrices are presented by Harvey (1974) and Folk (1972).

A variation of the cross-impact matrix that allows links directly to an institution's strategic emphases is force-field analysis. In a force-field analysis the institution identifies pressures (forces) and links them to the institution's planned responses. For example, a community college's planning team recommended four strategic emphases: (1) develop satellite centers; (2) change student recruiting to emphasize not just more, but different—more heterogeneous—students; (3) start an in-house faculty re-development program; and (4) expand the lifelong learning programs. These emphases responded to certain "forces" as illustrated in the left margin of Figure C.

While the cross-impact and probability-diffusion matrices illustrate national level changes (Figures A and B), they too can be taken down to the local level, just as I have illustrated how a community college analyzed its immediate environment with the force-field analysis (Figure C). Four levels of analysis are obviously possible with each of the techniques: world, national, state, and local. While Oxford and Harvard might profit most from a world-level analysis, Yakima Valley College and Metropolitan State College would profit most from a local analysis.

The translation of values into public policy is what politics is about.
—Willard Gaylin

2. Values Profiling

A second device for displaying anticipated changes is the values profile. Here we are trying to illustrate changes in socio-political value systems. Like the other approaches, this device, in chart form (see Figure D), should be viewed not as a precise measurement, but merely as one more useful way to consider changes in the environment.

Figure C

FORCE-FIELD ANALYSIS*

	Strategic Responses			
Forces →	Satellite Programing	Recruitment of Different Students	Faculty Development	Life Long Learning
85% Tenured Faculty			X	
Trend Toward Older Citizens in Community		X		X
Declining Number of High School Graduates		X		
Declining State Revenues	X		X	
Long-Term Residential Growth Occuring in Open Lands Away from Central Campus	X			
State and Local Push for Accountability			X	
Facility Capacity Underutilized in Afternoon and Evening		X		X
New Campus Presidential Style as Innovator	X			X
New Types of Industries		X		
Many Closed Elementary School Buildings	X			

*A community college

This chart is made up of contrasting value dimensions (enhancement of one value suggests diminution of the other) tending to shift as each new generation responds to changing conditions with shifting attitudes. Of course the change should illustrate the value changes most likely to occur among the segments of the population each college serves—or might serve.

This chart emphasizes value changes likely to occur in the segment of the population higher education has traditionally served—younger men and women coming from homes where there has been a tradition of higher education, of moderate affluence, and of "commitment" to causes. These men and women might be considered the trend setters, the harbingers of change among other segments of the population.

The chart shows two value profiles, present and near-future. The present line represents the approximate balance struck by these trend setters in the mid-1970s; the future line represents the approximate balance expected in the mid-1980s. The location of these balance points can be determined with some accuracy through a combination of survey research using Likert scales and the Delphi technique using a panel of experts—perhaps futurists.

Maintaining an awareness of the environment is a continuing process, the essence of which is the integration of the various forecasts. The four-sided conceptual framework used at the opening of this presentation may give the impression that there are only four sets of data to manage. How many sets of data there are depends on the definitions employed. It would be conceivable to have seven sides to the framework (economic, social, technological, political, legal, manpower, and financial), but I find that four is neater.

How many sets of probable events are examined is much less important than estimating the probability and importance of each event or pattern of events for a given college. Colleges should determine which trends have the combined highest ratings of probability and importance. Some events might have a high probability but be of low importance to the college. On the other hand, there might be some events of low probability but of high importance should they occur.

Perhaps the most carefully-worked-out scheme for assessing futures related to higher education is being tested now by the Resource Center for Planned Change of the American Association of State Colleges and Universities. They have developed a four-sided, cross-impact paradigm that integrates (1) national trends, (2) local trends, (3) values, and (4) institutional sectors. By institutional sectors, they refer to curricula,

Figure D

ESTIMATING VALUE-SYSTEM CHANGES
1980-1990

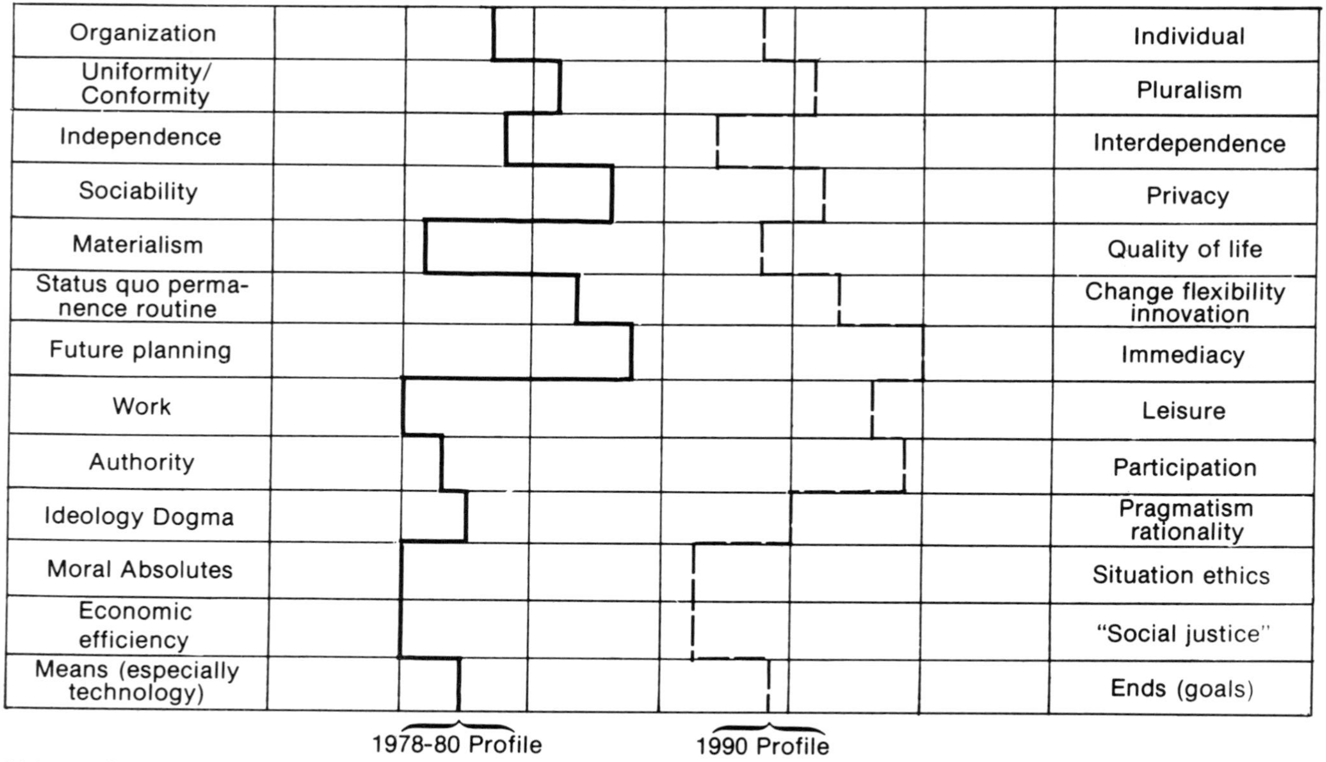

Organization	Individual
Uniformity/ Conformity	Pluralism
Independence	Interdependence
Sociability	Privacy
Materialism	Quality of life
Status quo perma-nence routine	Change flexibility innovation
Future planning	Immediacy
Work	Leisure
Authority	Participation
Ideology Dogma	Pragmatism rationality
Moral Absolutes	Situation ethics
Economic efficiency	"Social justice"
Means (especially technology)	Ends (goals)

1978-80 Profile 1990 Profile

*Adapted from: Ian H. Wilson, "Socio-Political Forecasting: A New Dimension to Strategic Planning," Michigan Business Review, July 1974, p.15-25.

faculty, students, public service, and so on. For details write to Kent Alm, One Dupont Circle NW, Suite 700, Washington DC 20036.

Other Colleges and Universities

Since an important part of the environment is occupied by other institutions, a more pointed environmental assessment examines the competition. The use of metropolitan Boston as an example, and the position of Boston University in particular as an illustration, demonstrates what presidents know all too well: Institutions must compete successfully to live at all.

Concentrated in the Boston Metropolitan Area are nearly 60 colleges and universities, nearly 50 of which are private. About 80% of the college attendance in the area is in the private sector. Boston University, a major institution in terms of both size (about 40,000 students) and constituent colleges, lies in the middle of America's most college-intense urban environment. North across the Charles River one can see the prestigious spires of both Harvard and MIT, and to the south is a five-square-mile plot of urban environment virtually carpeted with community colleges, a state college, several private liberal-arts colleges, business schools, and technical institutes.

Boston college is the quality institution for Boston's large Irish and Catholic populations. Brandeis is the impressive, richly-intellectual, Jewish-sponsored liberal-arts university. Northeastern University, the largest private institution in the country, sprawling and scattered over the Back Bay, dominates higher education's vocational-technical offerings. Tufts University is a smaller version of Boston University with a better-quality image, having its own co-ordinate college for women. And finally, among the major competitors, there is the public newcomer, the University of Massachusetts at Boston, with a tuition level about one-eighth that of Boston University.

Boston University operates one of three independent medical schools in greater Boston, and the University of Massachusetts has recently started a fourth medical school in Worcester: a reminder that not only do institutions compete, but their constituent units must compete as well. Witness the intense competition between California's public medical schools for students and federal funds.

It is obvious, then, why Boston University continues to attract a growing proportion of its regular day students from out of state, and even targets many of its summer offerings to attract adults from other Eastern and Midwestern urban settings, while the University's president has attempted to minimize the impression that public and private schools are so different that only public institutions should receive tax funds. Boston University, along with its constituent schools and colleges, probably presents the most difficult strategic-planning problem in the United States.

While the position of Boston University and its competitors is easy to see from a geographical perspective, it is less easy to reconcile the spatial position an institution occupies when considering a host of interacting variables such as tuition levels, nearness to consumers, quality of offerings, and size. There is, however, a study of 12 public and private colleges and universities in the Pacific Northwest that demonstrates the concept of strategic positioning rather well (Leister, 1975). The institutions included were three state four-year schools, three community colleges, four private four-year schools, one high school with an active vocational-technical program, and one urban private secretarial-bookeeping school. The institutions were chosen from among others in the immediate region by Pacific Lutheran University to reflect the significant competition as well as the range of educational offerings to potential students in the southern region of Puget Sound, surrounding the University.

The positioning concept employed in analyzing where Pacific Lutheran University "fit" in the "market place" involved asking samples of people to tell where they perceived each of the institutions to be along the dimensions of six variables: cost, nearness, size, safety, quality, and offerings. Through a multi-dimensions-scaling statistical technique it is possible to construct aggregate multi-dimensional perceptual maps, a simple form of which is shown in Figure E. The author's interpretation of the figure follows:

> At the right of Figure E, the University of Washington is viewed distinctly from the other institutions, but is closest to the other four-year state colleges. The four private four-year schools are perceived to be in close proximity to one another, as are the three community colleges. At the far left of the figure are found the vocational-technical school and the secretarial-bookkeeping school . . . the figure demonstrates the wide perceptual differences that exist among institutions and types (public/private/academic level) of institutions in competition with each other for the educational dollar in Western Washington. For example, psychological distance is greatest between the University of Washington (the largest single-campus university on the West Coast, with some 35,000 students) and the vocational-technical school. Many significant perceptual discriminations appear to exist between and among the 12 institutions. The careful observer will note even significant distinctions between institutions in the same general class, for example,

Figure E

PERCEPTUAL MAP OF INSTITUTIONAL MARKETS

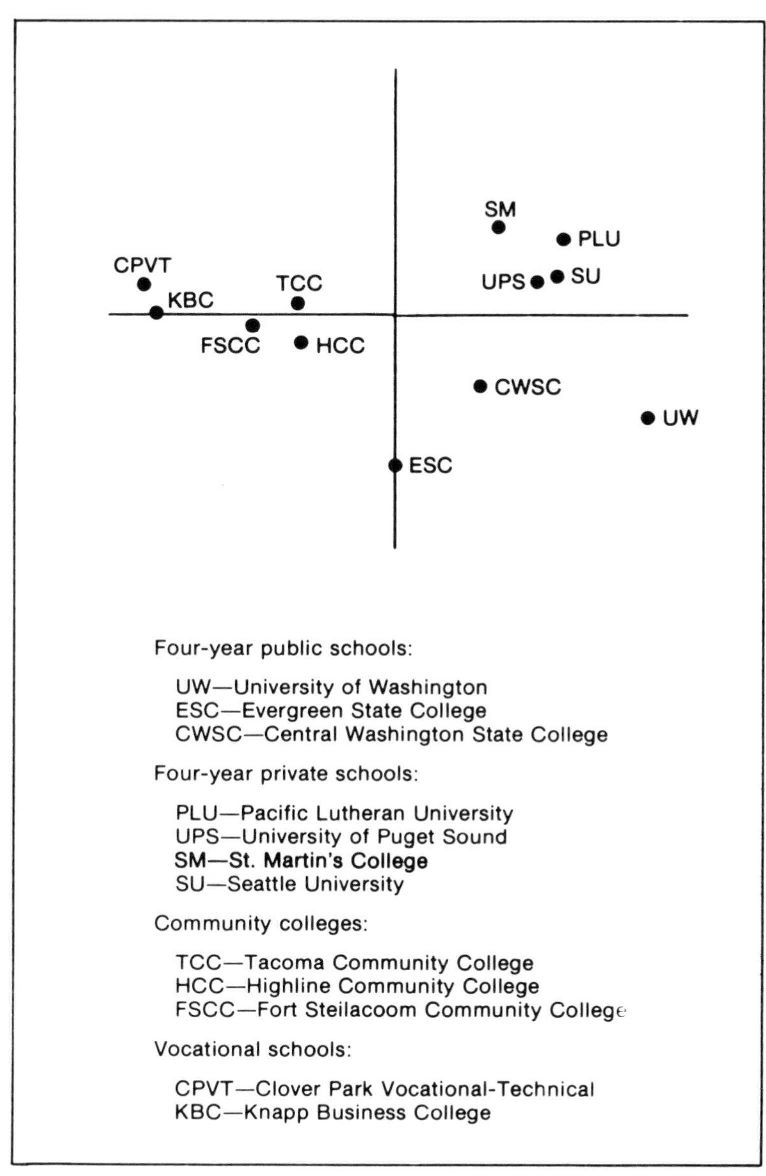

Source: Leister 1975

> among four-year public schools and among four-year private schools. For example, the educational innovativeness of the Evergreen State College (an open-concept school where students "contract" with faculty members for individualized courses of instruction) appears to have been recognized by the distinctive position it holds in the perceptual space.
>
> The perceptual map can be considered a visual model of the market structure of higher education in Western Washington as perceived by this sample of respondents. When constructed from the views of important target markets or persons likely to be influential in choice decisions, the maps can be considered devices for summarizing the degree of competition that exists between the institutions. Figure D clearly indicates that according to its present customers, PLU's closest competition comes from the other three private four-year schools, although it also must contend with CWSC and UW. (Leister, 1975, Page 391).

A slightly more complex way of looking at these same institutions is shown in Figure F. Here vectors for each characteristic indicate relative positions. The University of Washington (UW) is clearly highest on quality and variety of offerings, with Central Washington State College "average" on almost all vectors.[1]

Multi-dimensional scalings with joint space "maps" summarize a great deal of information that can be used in strategy formulations: the market position of competing institutions can be estimated; what is important in determining position on the map is brought out ; and the selection of a new position relative to the competition can be visualized. As Douglas Leister pointed out, these vector maps" . . . can be used as springboards for imagination regarding possible strategy alternatives. . . .(Leister, 1975, Page 397)

The uncertainty of the future has always made me look upon plans which need considerable time to carry them out as decoys for fools.

—*Jean-Jacques Rousseau*
Confessions

[1]Perpendicular lines drawn from each of the points (institutions) to the vector will rank the institutions on that particular characteristic. For example, the highest on the quality vector is the University of Washington (UW), followed by PLU, UPS, SU, SWSC, ESC, SM, HCC, FSCC, TCC, CPVT, KBC. The technique of analysis is from Paul E. Green and Vithala R. Rao, Applied Multi-dimensional Scaling, New York, Holt, Rinehart, and Winston, Inc., 1972.

Figure F

JOINT-SPACE MAP OF INSTITUTIONAL MARKET

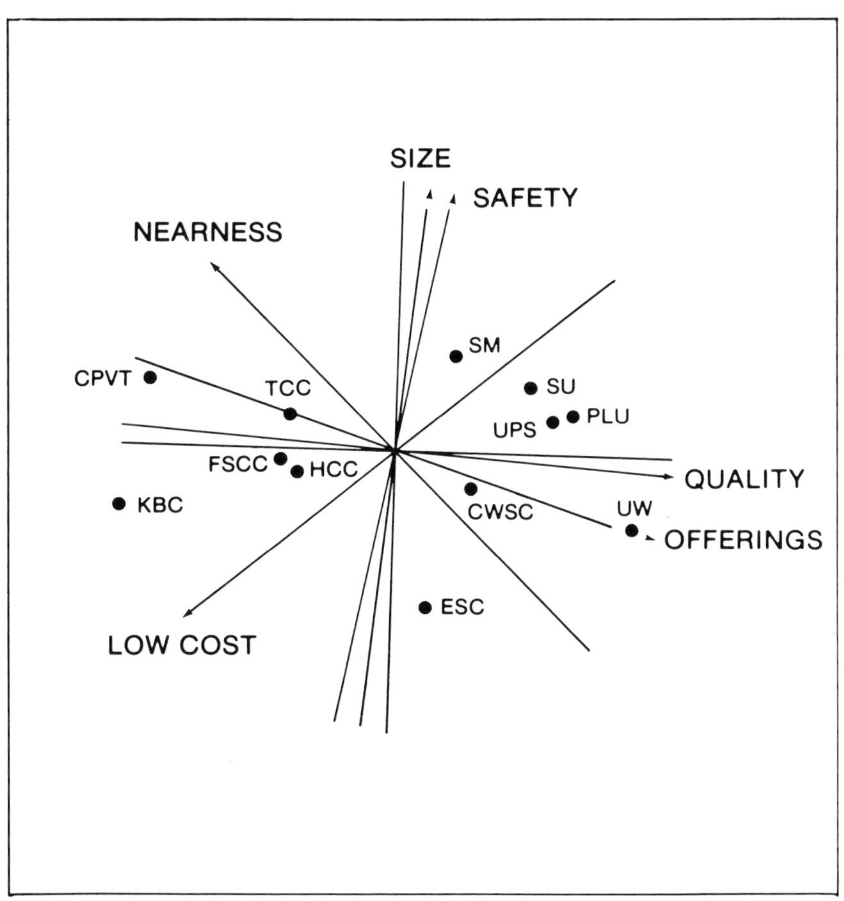

Source: Leister 1975

The Internal Environment of Values and Constraints

The analysis until now has focused on what might be called economic matters—the strengths and weaknesses of the college as they match the opportunities in the external environment. We have not considered, for example, the personal values of the institution's president or the conceptions of the institution's functions by other members of the institution—particularly the faculty. The chief executives have certain aims in life, just as the professional staff members hold norms and values relating to what they should do and how they should do it. These personal values and institutional beliefs usually harmonize with the optimum combinations of opportunities and strengths, and they must, since the key managers/administrators, faculty members, and even students must either contribute to or assent to strategic plans if these plans are to be effective. Thus the economic strategy should not conflict with the several sets of personal values or the institutional beliefs. Economic strategy, personal values, and institutional beliefs must be reconciled with one another.

Where personal values and institutional beliefs are not consistent with economic strategy, I do not suggest that they be denied or "ruled out of order". They should be accepted as a matter of course, and as far as possible economic strategy should be amended to accommodate these values. The challenge is to compose a strategic plan that merges three, rather than two, possibly-divergent sets of considerations into a single pattern. This may increase the complexity of the task, but the integrating process is the same: Starting with dominant or immovable considerations, we probe for the elements in conflict, looking for points which may be subject to adjustment. We are not carving a statue of marble so much as we are creating a work of kinetic art, the motion of which is determined by changes in the environment and the composition of the material itself.

The Analysts and Their Values

So far I have focused on the values held by central administrators and faculty members. The analyst, too, has some problems associated with values and how they influence the choice of data to highlight and the choice of purpose. The choice of purpose stems as much from the rational estimates of strengths and opportunities as it stems from the values of the analyst. Introspection is in order for several reasons. First, it may increase our tolerance when we see how others' formulations are clearly dictated by their values. Second, insights into our biases should pave the way for objective assessments of alternatives we do not feel could be right, so there is an examination of all the alternatives that may be available. And third, we may be forced to consider just how important it is to maintain a particular decision based on an unexpressed, unexamined, or unclear value.

Self-awareness will not immediately lead to the end of conflict as interest groups express themselves on the strategic formulations, but it will at least lessen unnecessary prolongation of differences. The analyst's goal is not to develop the unfailing ability to construct the perfectly-rational economic strategy and persuade others to accept it, but rather to acquire insight into the many-faceted problems of developing a plan that resolves the many potential views of what is right.

The process of developing a strategic plan is more effective when the following points are kept in mind:

1. Complete an analysis that links strengths to opportunities, testing all the time by the criteria identified in Chapter 5. How to do this is the subject of the next chapter.
2. Examine the plan.

3. Look to see to what extent the formulation coincides with the values held by the trustees, president, and faculty members, and to what extent it is consistent with what might be called the institutional beliefs. Remember that acceptance of strategic policy is necessary for implementation.

4. As an analyst, try to determine as far as possible what personal values are implicit in the recommended formulation.

5. As art is a human construction, so too is strategy. It must be in keeping with personal needs if it is to inspire commitment.

Conclusion

By going through a complete environmental assessment, one is likely to find evidence that the future will disclose an embarrassment of probable riches. To decide what is best among the opportunities available, however, requires more than an analysis of the environment. Since the essence of strategic planning is the fruitful match between environmental opportunities and restraints and institutional strengths and weaknesses, it is necessary to determine the college's distinctive competencies (what it can do particularly well) and limitations. The effort to identify competencies that are truly distinctive provides the important key to prioritizing goals and objectives. The best way to narrow the range of alternatives is to match the opportunities to distinctive competencies. That is the creative act providing the major challenge to today's central administrations, aided as they must be by appropriate analytical capacity with guidance and critiquing by faculty members. How to formulate the specifics of strategic policy is the subject of the next chapter.

Chapter 4

Planning is inseparable from management, and both involve those elements we associate with art—intuition, creativity, discernment, command of the work tools and materials, an appreciation of the interaction of form and function.
—Harold Enarson

FORMULATING A STRATEGIC PLAN

This is the how-to-do-it chapter. How to formulate strategic decisions. How to prioritize. How to go through a strategic planning process.

Consistent with the presentation in the earlier chapters, I wish to stress again that these decisions cannot be determined through exacting quantitative methods or any finite techniques which might, say through management science, be applied to narrower questions. Strategic decisions cannot be made with, for example, decisions rules. The decision makers and recommenders must have confidence in personal judgments, seasoned by analysis of similar questions, made with the knowledge that more than one good decision is possible. After all, there is seldom a single right answer.

Ultimately, strategic decisions should favor imaginative outcomes. The formulation process is essentially a creative activity. And as a creative activity, it is amenable to a number of mental skills and disciplines used in creative problem solving. Three such methods are discussed: Synthetics, lateral thinking, and brainstorming. I suggest that planning groups use these methods as plans are formulated.

Formulating the plan also involves obtaining the views from and seeking consensus among diverse members of an academic community. Two structured devices useful in seeking input and perhaps approaching consensus are also examined as part of the case examples: Education Testing Service's Institutional Goals Inventory and the Delphi Technique.

The chapter also presents as examples the planning processes employed at the University of Washington and the College of St. Benedict. Finally, a step-by-step process is outlined for the consideration of anyone given the responsibility of planning.

Team Approaches to Creative Problem Solving: Synectics, Brainstorming, and Lateral Thinking

Synectics, a term "Anglicized" from a Greek word meaning the joining together of apparently-unconnected elements, is a team approach for stimulating creative thought. It is basically a simple method, relying on a problem-solving sequence starting with a rigorous definition of the problem and proceeding to a separation of imaginative thinking from analytical and judgmental thinking. Its particular novelty is its forced withdrawal from the problem, during which an apparently-unrelated tangent is explored in free association which provides new ideas for solving the problem that attention has been drawn away from.

Synectics utilizes a team. Six is thought to be an ideal number. The members should be drawn from different parts of the campus: schools, departments, administrators, student leaders. Several or many teams can work on the planning problems simultaneously. These formulations can be compared. My experience suggests that no two groups will formulate the same general plan—a tribute to the possibilities and ingenuity involved.

Each team should be guided by a skilled leader—someone widely experienced, optimistic, and mature who is able to maintain sensitivity to each member's contributions and who understands the Synectics process.[1] This leader should have expert knowledge about those aspects of the college's operations essential to evaluating planning options the group might "dream up", but must not dominate the team. The leader may contribute ideas, but should give precedence to the ideas generated by others.

Gordon (1961) and Whitfield (1975) call attention on one hand to the need for the expert who knows the campus and its environment well, so that ideas may be evaluated against valid criteria, but are concerned on the other hand that such experienced people are more likely to be rigid in their thoughts, based as they are on a buildup of many years of self-reinforcing impressions, and are thus more likely to see only those future directions that fit the framework of their past experience. Nevertheless, they are valuable members of any team, since they can judge novel approaches against their background. It is a matter of awareness on the part of the expert who recognizes the need for balance.

---

[1]The headquarters of Synectics, Inc. is at 26 Church Street, Cambridge, Massachusetts. Synectics is a registered service mark of the Corporation. Probably the best source of information beyond writing to Synectics, Inc. is George Prince's book <u>The Practice of Creativity</u>, New York: Harper and Row, 1970.

The first step in a Synectics approach is to have the team members recognize that they are to recommend alternative futures, alternative statements on what the college is to be. It is helpful to have each team member state the task, each in his or her own way, after which initial ideas should be invited, built on, and perhaps assessed, but gently. At this point the emphasis is on the production of ideas; later a rigorous evaluation may take place.

It is after a substantial number of options have been suggested, and the generation of new options is slowing, that the novelty of the Synectics method asserts itself. The leader diverts attention from the planning objectives by taking the group on an "excursion", an intended "side trip", or a "vacation". This is a period of free discussion on a subject that would appear unrelated to determining the college's future course(s). The area chosen for discussion is not random. It is chosen because it might provide relevant analogies. Conceptual distance is important and seems to be provided by observations on the world of biology, since natural systems have found countless ways of adaptation, providing a rich source of living-organism-to-environment analogous problems and solutions: a robin's keen sense of hearing so it can find worms just below the surface, the radar of a bat, the cold light of a firefly. . . . After the excursion—which according to Prince (1972) should last from a few to as many as 15 minutes—attention is brought back to the planning problem and the team is asked to apply some of the ideas just discussed to strategic planning. Again speculation is encouraged and avenues are explored until inspiration runs out, at which point another excursion may be taken, perhaps with a new person leading the team.

A second kind of vacation-generating analogy found useful for new insights is to have team members assume the position of other significant actors in the environment who might imagine looking at the institution from their role-playing perspective, imagining what the college might be doing to serve their interest. Members become farm owners, doctors, housewives, city workers, colleagues at other institutions, and so on. Such personal views from "outside" vantage points are likely to generate new possibilities not easily seen by members of the "permanent" staff. To add even more reality to the "outside" view, it is possible to invite real farm owners, doctors, housewives, city workers, colleagues, and so on to Synectics sessions. Having outsiders view the strategic-planning possibilities is beneficial not only because of the special experience they bring from different fields, but also because they are not bogged down by the particular views that those within the institution have developed.

Team members must support each other so that fragile brain-children may have maximum possible nurturance before hard evaluating is done. One way to guard newer ideas is to impose a rule requiring a member of the team to recognize two or perhaps three aspects of a colleague's idea as good before beginning criticism. Requiring the critic to review the novel idea favorably may open his mind and other minds long enough for the idea to gain additional acceptance. Creativity should be the central concern.

Lateral Thinking

According to Edward de Bono (1975)[2] there are two sorts of thinking: "lateral thinking" and "vertical thinking". De Bono observed that in vertical thinking progress is made by following logical steps along a pathway, while in lateral thinking thought follows an uncommon path not dictated by logic and perhaps full of surprises, often resulting in unexpectedly-good solutions. His book contains an analogy of the flow of water along well-defined channels: The more it flows the deeper the channels, and the deeper the channels the more the flow is contained. That is vertical thinking. Lateral thinking is analogous to damming the old channels and cutting new channels to see where the water will go—perhaps nowhere useful—perhaps somewhere that will create a whole new pattern.

Do Bono does not claim that lateral thinking has any "magic" about it. He simply sees it as a disciplined mechanism for freeing the mind from habitual solutions, especially in those instances in which no solution seems available or in which a new view of an old situation is needed. He says: "Lateral thinking is for generating ideas. Logical thinking is for developing, selecting, and using them."

The principles of lateral thinking can be considered in four general and non-exclusive ways. Each may be considered a technique useful either by an individual (de Bono's intent) or in group processes:

1. Introduction of the intermediate impossible

To break the grip of vertical (logical) thinking, an "intermediate impossible" is introduced as a stepping stone between the easily-recognized problem and its easily-seen "solutions". Although unthinkable, the intermediate impossible must be related to the problem. For example:

---

[2]The Use of Lateral Thinking, Penguin Books, 1975. Earlier editions published by Jonathon Cape (1967) and Pelican Books (1971), both of Britain. The edition I have says it is not for sale in the USA, but there must be a publisher making it available in the United States.

"How can community-education services be made more efficient?" The intermediate impossible might be "All services must be offered by an agency other than the college." Ideas can be stimulated by this. Another intermediate impossible might be "The recipient of such services must remain stationary." The idea is to introduce outrageous possibilities to stimulate productive, innovative possibilities. Anything is a possible stimulant. Keep the unthinkable related to planning in the institution's environment: Sell half the academic programs to the locale's largest employer; open seven new campuses next year; take over a small college three states away; don't use the faculty for teaching. . . .

2. Introduction of random juxtaposition

This is another way of finding a stepping stone, involving the introduction of a random concept to spark new associations. The random juxtaposition is like the Synectics excursion into an unrelated area in search of appropriate analogies. Using the same question cited above ("How can community education services be offered more efficiently?"), The lateral-thinking group might open a thesaurus anywhere, finding (say) the word "courage", which I did. Exploring I found such synonyms as bravery, valor, intrepidity, dash, self-reliance, spunk, and bold stroke, and such adjectives as heart-of-oak, intrepid, plucky, audacious, spirited, and so on. Dash? Could advertising be changed to have more dash and thus attract more attention? Spirited? Could an effort be made to offer more spirited instruction to adults who have worked all day? Self-reliance? Could community education emphasize courses on self-reliance?

Seven planning-team members, each armed with a thesaurus or dictionary and each examining the contents for stimulating word associations, can come up with many ideas. The group will need all the writing space that can be provided—pads, chalkboards, flip charts, butcher paper. . . .

3. Search for different ways of looking at the problem

With respect to getting a clearer view of, for example, the challenge to come up with a strategic plan, one approach is to state the purpose the plan is to fulfill and then examine each part of that purpose in detail. I have said: "The purpose of strategic planning is to determine the pattern of objectives, purposes, goals, and major policies and plans for achieving these goals stated in such a way as to define what the college is or is to become." Challenging this purpose systematically we might say: Determine? Why determine at all? Why have a pattern? Why seek achievement of goals? Is it necessary to define? Is it necessary to believe it should continue to be a college? Maybe some other institution could be created?

The objective of rotating around the purpose served by the plan in this way is to provide a better appreciation of the plan and a firmer basis for stimulating fresh ideas. Each aspect of the plan itself should then be rotated, examined, and clarified to find out what the essentials are. Any apparent restraints that seem inescapable should likewise be rotated, examined, and clarified, and thus not be taken for granted. The familiar and apparently-successful programs of the college should not be allowed to dominate; they too should be rotated, examined, challenged. . . .

4.Use of chance

To quote Edward de Bono: "It may seem paradoxical to suggest that something can be done about chance, for by definition chance events cannot be brought about by any design. That is precisely their value in leading to new ideas." (de Bono, 1975, Page 94)

While de Bono advances "chance" as a separate basic principle in the generation of new ideas, I find the concept sufficiently like random juxtaposition and similar both to the outcomes of the intermediate impossible and to the "search" that I question the appropriateness of its being considered a fourth principle. Nevertheless, de Bono introduces some techniques to increase the likelihood that chance associations will come to mind. Included among these is emphasizing the value of playing without design or direction.

> The very usefulness of play is its greatest asset. It is freedom from design or commitment that allows chance to juxtapose things which otherwise would not have been arranged. . .to construct a sequence of events that would not otherwise have been constructed. . . . During play ideas suggest themselves and then breed further ideas. Pages 98-99)

A second way to enhance chance is to wander around a place that is full of things, full of stimulants.

> A general store, or an exhibition, or even a library could provide such a setting, and it is more useful if the setting is not directly appropriate. Nothing deliberately looked for, but instead of a searching attitude there is a readiness to consider anything that attracts the attention. Often it is the most

> irrelevant objects that are capable of stimulating the mind toward a new idea. (Page 99)

Perhaps a planning committee should simply take time now and then to wander about bookshops, a Salvation Army second-hand store, a department store, or an antique shop. Any "rich" environment could spark imagination. An unsought-after stimulus can set off useful trains of ideas.

> *Creativity is so delicate a flower that praise tends to make it bloom, while discouragement often nips it in the bud. Any of us will put out more and better ideas if our efforts are appreciated.*
> *—Alex F. Osborn*

Brainstorming

The third method, brainstorming, is probably the simplest and oldest approach for generating fresh ideas in group settings. Ideas are contributed in a setting in which it is insisted that certain rules be followed, rules that allow spontaneous expression:

1. No criticism of any idea should be allowed. Judgments should come later.
2. All ideas, no matter how wild or frivolous, should be welcomed.
3. The production of the greatest number of ideas should be encouraged.
4. Creating chain reactions of ideas—ideas building on ideas should be encouraged.

In a relaxed environment in which it is safe for people to think freely and adventurously, ideas cannot be "destroyed" since analysis and judgments are expressly forbidden. It is possible—indeed encouraged—for other people's ideas to be taken and improved on. A healthy rivalry in the production of ideas can develop.

Brainstorming sessions should develop many tentative planning options for later development, and still later analysis. The first sessions should provide an atmosphere for roaming free, for indulging in fantasy. The best ideas should be summarized and subjected to a second round of sessions in which each idea should still be supported and filled out, again in a supportive atmosphere. Only in later sessions should critiquing be more severe and tests such as those suggested in Chapter 5 applied.

Alex Osborn (1953), who is credited with originating the systematic application and study of brainstorming in the late 1930s, provides some additional guidelines. The group should be led by someone who has had some experience with the technique and who can maintain the special discipline needed. There should be a recorder—either an electronic recorder or someone to make a record of the ideas. A balanced team of perhaps a dozen with some self-starters and a few deep thinkers with a variety of backgrounds will provide about the right mixture. Clique formation must be avoided so that the group will act as a unified team. The leader must apply the rules firmly.

Before the group attempts the main objective of formulating planning alternatives, some short practice sessions may be arranged using any of the college's problems, especially if the group is not familiar with the technique.

A time limit is useful to spur members to come up with ideas before the time runs out. An hour is suggested. Some people will naturally produce ideas, and perhaps these will even be written out. They should only be allowed to present them one at a time, so all the participants can have an opportunity to build on each idea separately.

When the right atmosphere is achieved, the participants can be expected to generate a flood of ideas which will come in a pattern. The first flow of ideas will be fairly obvious given that college's familiar setting: Reach a student population a bit different from that now served; appeal to adults; add certain new degree programs; combine the efforts of certain faculty groups, and the like. Then the flow of ideas will trickle, but there will be a change in quality as increasingly-novel ideas are expressed and as minds wander farther afield and begin searching in less-familiar ways. Often the best ideas will occur at those moments when the trickle has nearly dried up. Often ideas will begin flowing again after a break.

Meeting Places for Enhancing Imaginative Thought

The meeting place is an important consideration. There should be plenty of paper around: on the walls, on flip-chart stands, in pads on stands beside the participants—who whould not sit around a table, particularly a square or rectangular table. The room itself should be in a neutral setting, away from the trappings of central administration, faculty, or student life. Everyting possible should be done to create an atmosphere free of pressures leading to conformity. Individuals should be free to experiment, to build on each others' ideas, to be wrong.

Even though it has a table (and a useful one, too), I am impressed with a particular room used by planning groups (and individuals) at the Weyerhaeuser Company. This room was largely the idea of Wayne Gaughran, one of the Company's managers, and was built expressly for innovative problem solving and action. Except for some small windows and a large map of the world, the walls are covered with expanses of paper. There are dry markers everywhere to be used on the blank flip charts which are both on the walls and on movable stands. There are sliding panels all along one wall, three deep, effectively providing for three walls on one. One wall holds a vertically-mounted roll of yard-wide butcher paper, so it is possible to start composing ideas on a three-by-twelve-foot (36-square-foot!) sheet of paper. In all there are over 100 square feet of blank paper on the walls and on the flip charts. Everyone can join in as ideas flow. There is also a picture screen, a telephone, and a large round table. The setting is excellent for innovating, participative thinking, and participants can take the ideas with them, on the paper, when they leave.

Examples of planning using consensus-seeking devices

The University of Houston allowed nearly two years for a study of its future. The emphasis of the study was on data about the institution and its environment; however one part of that investigation was to assess the internal values held with regard to the mission of the university.[3] The basic survey instrument chosen for assessing values held by faculty members, administrators, students, and alumni was the Institutional Goals Inventory developed by Educational Testing Service. The Inventory was developed by ETS to assist colleges and universities in delineating goals so that these could be used for determining priorities for action. There are 90 statements on the Inventory, leading to 20 goals.

A brief description of the 20 goals appears in Figure G. The University modified the Inventory provided by ETS by adding 10 statements that were deemed particularly important to the University in Houston. Respondents evaluate statements on the basis of two criteria: (1) how important the goal is at the institution at the present time and how important it should be at this institution; and (2) how important the goal is to the institution. A part of the questionnaire is illustrated in Figure H.

The results were displayed in tables such as that in Figure I for the benefit of a Steering Committee which was appointed to design and direct the total study, and nine other task committees each responsible to the Steering

[3]For more detail see Robert C. Shirley, "Information Inputs to Decisions on University Mission", in Robert Cope (editor), Information for Decisions in Post-secondary Education, Association for Institutional Research, 1975, 355-360.

Figure G

BRIEF DESCRIPTION OF INSTITUTIONAL GOAL INVENTORY SCALES

Outcome Goals:

1. Academic Development (acquisition of knowledge, high intellectual standards)
2. Intellectual Orientation (attitude toward learning, commitment to life-long personal development)
3. Individual Personal Development (enhancement of self-concept, identification of personal goals)
4. Humanism/Altruism (social and moral concerns related to the welfare of man, world peace)
5. Cultural/Aesthetic Awareness (appreciation of the arts)
6. Traditional Religiousness (dedication to serving God)
7. Vocational Preparation (training for specific careers, re-training opportunities)
8. Advanced Training (providing graduate and professional educational opportunities)
9. Research (conducting basic research, advancing knowledge)
10. Meeting Local Needs (providing continuing education opportunities, trained manpower for local employers)
11. Public Service (helping the disadvantaged, assisting governmental agencies, solving social problems)
12. Social Egalitarianism (providing remedial programs, assistance to minorities)
13. Social Criticism/Activism (critical evaluation of society and its institutions, orientation toward change)

Process Goals:

14. Freedom (ensuring both academic and personal freedoms)
15. Democratic Governance (providing for faculty and student participation in governance)
16. Community (maintaining climate of openness and trust)
17. Intellectual/Aesthetic Environment (providing an intellectually exciting campus)
18. Innovation (developing new approaches to learning, grading)
19. Off-Campus Learning (awarding academic credit for off-campus study)
20. Accountability/Efficiency (using cost criteria to evaluate program alternatives, concern for efficiency)

Figure H

EXAMPLE FROM DIRECTIONS TO INSTITUTIONAL GOAL INVENTORY*

DIRECTIONS

The *Inventory* consists of 90 statements of possible institutional goals. Using the answer key shown in the examples below, you are asked to respond to each statement in two different ways:

First – How important *is* the goal at this institution at the present time?

Then – In your judgment, how important *should* the goal *be* at this institution?

EXAMPLES

		of no importance or not applicable	of low importance	of medium importance	of high importance	of extremely high importance
A. to require a common core of learning experiences for all students...	is	○	○	○	○	●
	should be	○	○	●	○	○

In this example, the respondent believes the goal "to require a common core of learning experiences for all students" is presently of extremely high importance, but thinks that it should be of medium importance.

		of no importance or not applicable	of low importance	of medium importance	of high importance	of extremely high importance
B. to give alumni a larger and more direct role in the work of the institution...	is	○	●	○	○	○
	should be	○	○	○	●	○

In this example, the respondent sees the goal "to give alumni a larger and more direct role in the work of the institution" as presently being of low importance, but thinks that it should be of high importance.

- Unless you have been given other instructions, consider the institution as a whole in making your judgments.
- In giving *should be* responses, do not be restrained by your beliefs about whether the goal, realistically, can ever be attained on the campus.
- Please try to respond to every goal statement in the *Inventory*, by blackening one oval after *is* and one oval after *should be*.
- Use any soft lead pencil. Do not use colored pencils or a pen–ink, ball point, or felt tip.
- Mark each answer so that it completely fills (blackens) the intended oval. Please do not make checks (√) or X's.

*Used with permission of Educational Testing Service.

Figure I

GOAL AREA "IS" AND "SHOULD BE" MEANS*

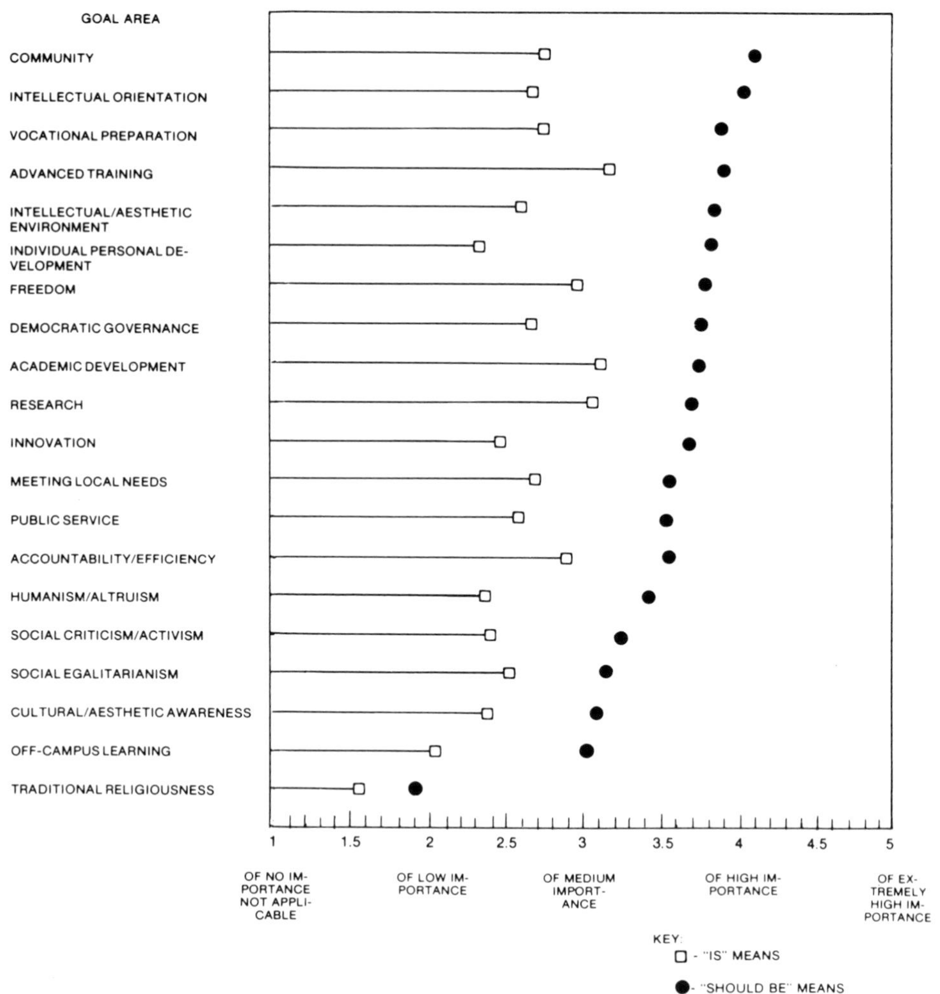

*From Robert Shirley, "Information Inputs to Decisions on University Mission," in Cope (ed.), Information for Decisions in Postsecondary Education, 1975, p. 357.

Committee. All the committees operated on the premise that the goals should be a function of: (1) environmental needs and opportunities, (2) environmental constraints, (3) internal resources and capabilities, and (4) internal values.

Australian National University

The Australian National University (ANU), wanting to know how faculty members, administrators, students, and support-staff members viewed organizational priorities, modified the Institutional Goals Inventory in accordance with the analysis of university goal systems by Richman and Farmer presented in their Leadership Goals and Power in Higher Education (1974). The resulting questionnaire had 32 goal statements in response to which each respondent was asked to indicate: (a) his or her belief as to the importance of, or the emphasis on, that goal in the ANU at the time; and (b) his or her judgment or preference as to how important that goal should be.

The intent of the study (personal correspondence) was "to take a first look in the mirror with a view to tidying up its (ANU's) appearance".

The results of the survey were largely "comforting" internally, as there was a high degree of agreement among diverse faculty groups, administrators, students, and even less-involved support-staff members on the perceived importance of priorities. The survey thus provided a reasonable base of common understanding for further analysis.

The cover letter and formats of the questionnaire are illustrated in Figures J and K. Copies of the complete questionnaire can be obtained from Allen Miller (see cover letter).

The major shortcoming of this study was the inadequacy of the follow-through, which consisted simply of a not-for-the-public summary report provided for the University community as a discussion paper. Similar but better approaches are illustrated next—better because of greater involvement of the academic community along with specific post-study links to action programs.

The Delphi Technique

An important way of obtaining ideas for a planning effort as well as obtaining some degree of consensus from members of the academic community is to use a variation of the Delphi Technique. Because no single

Figure J

COVER LETTER FOR UNIVERSITY GOAL SURVEY

THE AUSTRALIAN NATIONAL UNIVERSITY

Box 4 P.O. Canberra A.C.T. 2600   Telephone 49-5111   Telegrams and Cables Natunis Canberra

OFFICE FOR RESEARCH IN ACADEMIC METHODS   Telephone 4594/2669

IN REPLY PLEASE QUOTE

A University-wide Study of Goals and Objectives

Any complex organisation has multiple goals. Universities are no exception and the ANU is the most complex university in the country. Leadership and decision-making in the University need to be guided by clearly understood goals and objectives - the more so in times of restricted funds when decisions about priorities have to be made, at both government and university levels. What are the goals or intentions of the ANU?

What appear to be goals from the point of view of administration may not be goals at all from the point of view of those in class rooms, laboratories and workshops; and what may be more important, what we see as our goals may not be what those outside the University want from it. If dictation of goals from the outside is to be resisted we must be clear what our goals are, and divergences among us must be understood and, if possible, resolved.

With the approval of the Vice-Chancellor, the Office for Research in Academic Methods is conducting a wide-ranging survey of goals and objectives as they are seen and understood by all members of the ANU community. Will you assist this inquiry by completing the questionnaire which accompanies this letter? This invitation is being extended to every member of the ANU community. If every member will respond, we shall have the best possible basis for knowing what the most desirable goals are. We shall have begun to strengthen the University's justification of the national and community resources invested in it and required to maintain it.

These questionnaires are being distributed in such a way that sections of the ANU community will be identifiable, but each individual is anonymous. You may, however, indicate your willingness to be identified by signing the response sheet. ORAM would appreciate signed returns for the opportunity they would give for follow-up interviews where it seems these may clarify issues raised. No report of the study will identify any individual member with any particular response.

Allen H. Miller
Head of ORAM

C. A. Gibb
Visiting Fellow

Figure K

EXAMPLE FROM UNIVERSITY GOAL SURVEY

Please respond to these goal statements by marking one X after is and one after should be.

			of no importance or not applicable	of low importance	of medium importance	of high importance	of extremely high importance
1.	to contribute through research to the general advancement of knowledge...	*is*					
		should be					
2.	to help students acquire depth of knowledge in at least one academic discipline...	*is*					
		should be					
3.	to train students in methods of scholarly inquiry, scientific research and/or problem definition and solution...	*is*					
		should be					
4.	to help students understand and respect people from diverse backgrounds and cultures...	*is*					
		should be					
5.	to promote general powers of the mind — the aim being to produce not mere specialists but cultivated men and women...	*is*					
		should be					
6.	to maintain high quality in a balanced way in all teaching and research programmes...	*is*					
		should be					
7.	to maintain top quality in a few designated important programmes...	*is*					
		should be					
8.	to create an overall system of university decision-making that is genuinely responsive to the concerns of all members of the university...	*is*					
		should be					
9.	to provide critical evaluations of prevailing practices and values in Australian society...	*is*					
		should be					
10.	to move to a policy of essentially open admissions, and then to develop meaningful educational experiences for all who are admitted...	*is*					
		should be					
11.	to provide opportunities for continuing education for adults in the local area...	*is*					
		should be					
12.	to produce students who will be objective and constructive in their thinking about the problems of society...	*is*					
		should be					
13.	to encourage members of the academic community to give primary loyalty to the university rather than to a discipline or profession...	*is*					
		should be					
14.	to maintain a continuous and steady rate of growth of the university...	*is*					
		should be					
15.	to create an institution known widely as an intellectually exciting and stimulating place...	*is*					
		should be					
16.	to admit preferably high quality students who may be expected to achieve high levels of academic success...	*is*					
		should be					

way of proceeding is recommended, I will simply provide examples from some better applications.

Mount St. Mary's College (Los Angeles) began the implementation of an Exxon-supported Resource Allocation Management Program (RAMP) in 1975 with a two-day goals workshop. The faculty and administrators at that workshop came up with a list of 53 possible goals. The 53 goal statements were then circulated among administrators, faculty members and a sample of students for assessment. A portion of the opinionnaire is illustrated in Figure L. The opinionnaire also provided space to list new goals not mentioned at the workshop. The new goals would be assessed in a third and final round of assessment, again via opinionnaire.

Figure M illustrates the cover letter and the first page of the survey form used for ranking a final list of 28 "top ranked" goals. And finally Figure N illustrates the three-page final report to participants.

The advantages of Mount St. Mary's approach included: (1) the speed at which it was done (about five months); (2) the degree of openness (all new suggestions had a hearing); (3) the relevance of the goals to Mount St. Mary's situation (rather than using an all-purpose goal survey); (4) the clear linking of this exercise to resource allocation; and (5) the link at the end to task forces which would be given responsibility and direct access to the president's office for implementation.

While the examples from the University of Houston, the Australian National University (ANU) and Mount St. Mary's College illustrate diverse approaches to identifying goals and means of seeking some consensus, the resulting statements are all too broad to help determine how resources should be allocated—positioned in the strategic sense.

A planning effort at the University of Santa Clara attempted to avoid the generality of the goals arrived at by Houston, ANU, and Mount St. Mary's by having its 26-member Community Council use ideas from the 11-college study by Ladd (1970), and adding local issues to develop a list of goals with more operational substance. The point is well put by Robert Pardon (1972):

> When a goal inventory is completed, not only should it provide a priority ranking as perceived by those who contribute to the consensus, but the individual statements should describe the action to be taken. (Page 106)

Figure L

EXAMPLES FROM DELPHI OPINIONNAIRE

GOALS STUDY
Round Two

Sept. - Oct. 1975

Mount St. Mary's College

Please check the appropriate column to indicate whether or not you agree that the action described is a goal which the Mount St. Mary's College community should work together to achieve over the next three to five years.

		Strongly Agree	Agree	Undecided	Disagree
1.	To reaffirm and find ways of making manifest the Catholicity of MSMC.				
2.	To reaffirm and find ways of making manifest the College's commitment to the education of women.				
3.	To study whether MSMC should emphasize its programs designed primarily for women or continue to expand as a coeducational institution.				
4.	To clarify what we mean in saying MSMC is a "liberal arts college," and then align the learning environment and academic program with this definition.				
5.	To reaffirm and find ways of making manifest MSMC's commitment to quality education; develop yardstick for measuring quality of MSMC's educational program.				
6.	To identify and implement the means for better communication among students, faculty, staff, alumnae, and administration.				
7.	To identify and implement means for increasing MSMC's visibility within the Los Angeles community.				
8.	To identify and implement ways of bringing the resources of the college to the Los Angeles community, and of availing ourselves of the resources of the community.				
10.	To promote a spirit of unity among faculty and students on both campuses.				

COVER LETTER AND FIRST PAGE FOR RANKING GOALS

MOUNT ST. MARY'S COLLEGE

To: Participants in MSMC's Goals Study 1975

From: Barbara Becker

Date: November 17, 1975

The third and final round of our Goals Study is attached. (To refresh memories: Round One consisted of group discussions on September 2, and produced fifty-three possible goals; in Round Two you were asked to indicate how strongly you agreed or disagreed with the goals suggested.)

Now, in Round Three you are being asked to rank those goals which occasioned the strongest agreement from second-round respondents. (Of the 227 opinionnaires distributed to faculty, administrative staff, participating trustees, regents, and alumnae, and a random sample of students, 110 were completed and returned.) Space is provided for you to indicate the ten goals you think should have top priority over the next three to five years.

In addition, you are asked to give some consideration to the means to be used to achieve your top-priority goals, and where the primary responsibility should lie. For instance, *if* we had agreed upon the goal "To develop an honor system at the College," the major responsibility for achieving this goal might lie with one of the Student Government bodies, or with the Dean of Students Office, or with some committee. It will be helpful, however, to our January task of examining present decision-making structures if we know who you perceive as having the primary responsibility for moving MSMC toward the achievement of those goals ranked among your top ten.

Early in 1976 all of the final goals in rank order will be published to the college community and submitted to Sister Cecilia Louise for formal approval by the Board of Trustees. Subsequently, we will have to engage in the setting of measureable objectives leading to the achievement of these goals.

The DEADLINE for this round is FRIDAY, DECEMBER 12. Please return your opinionnaire to the Goals Study box in the foyer of Building 7 on the Doheny campus, or Box 72 or H-411 on the Chalon campus.

Thank you for your continued cooperation--and thoughtful response.

Nov. - Dec. 1975

GOALS STUDY
Round Three
Page 1

MOUNT ST. MARY'S COLLEGE

In the far-left column, please rank the ten goals which you think should have top priority over the next three to five years. Place a 1 beside the goal you consider most important, a 2 beside your second choice, etc. The larger middle and righthand columns are optional, although it would be most helpful if you would give some consideration to means and responsibility. Wherever you have ideas regarding the means to achieve and the assignation of responsibility for a goal ranked among your ten, please take time to write in these ideas--but do not neglect to return your opinionnaire just because these two columns are blank. The far-left column is the most important for your completion. Thank you!

Rank	GOAL	Means to be used to achieve this goal	Person, department, or committee who should assume responsibility
____	1. To reaffirm and find ways of making manifest MSMC's commitment to quality education; develop yardstick for measuring quality of MSMC's educational program.		
____	2. To identify and implement the means for better communication among students, faculty, staff, alumnae, and administration.		
____	3. To identify and implement means for increasing MSMC's visibility within the Los Angeles community.		
____	4. To identify and implement ways of bringing the resources of the college to the Los Angeles community, and of availing ourselves of the resources of the community.		

FINAL REPORT ON DELPHI SURVEY

MOUNT ST. MARY'S COLLEGE

To: Participants in MSMC's GOALS STUDY 1975
From: Barbara Becker
Date: January 12, 1976
Re: Final Report

Thanks to your cooperation we have completed the process initiated to engage the college community in establishing MSMC's Goals for the next three to five years. As you recall, this process began with group discussions on Sept. 2, from which came fifty-three possible goals. In the second round opinionnaire you were asked to indicate how strongly you agreed or disagreed with these fifty-three suggested goals. Finally, in the third round you were asked to rank, from the goals eliciting strongest agreement in Round Two, those ten you thought should have top priority. You were also requested to recommend means to be used to achieve the goals to which you gave top priority, and where primary responsibility for the achievement of these goals should lie.

On the basis of the ninety-five opinionnaires returned, the following goals have found strongest support within the campus community and have been selected by Sister Cecilia Louise for priority effort during the coming three to five years:

GOAL 1 - To expand efforts to attract more students for departments other than nursing (which already has a full quota of students). (555 points)

GOAL 2 - To reaffirm and find ways of making manifest MSMC's commitment to quality education; to develop a yardstick for measuring the quality of MSMC's educational program. (456 points)

GOAL 3 - To identify and tap additional resources, both financial and other. (389 points)

GOAL 4 - To develop means by which to upgrade faculty salaries in order to recruit and retain good faculty. (373 points)

GOAL 5 - To reaffirm and find ways of making manifest the Catholicity/Christianity of MSMC. (357 points)

GOAL 6 - To identify and implement means for increasing MSMC's visibility within the Los Angeles community. (335 points)

All other goals received less than three-hundred points. Ranking of the goals was established on a point system incorporating both times ranked and rank placement. (A goal ranked 1st on an opinionnaire received eleven points: one for being selected and ten for being ranked first; whereas a goal ranked 8th received only four points: one for being selected and three for being ranked eighth.)

p. 2

In order to capitalize on the manifest interest in these goals and the wide range of talents and energies within this academic community, six task forces (one for each goal) will be formed to expedite the achievement of these goals. Reporting directly to the President, these groups will have as their Spring '76 semester tasks:

- to refine the goal as stated
- to clarify the present situation within the goal-related area
- to identify means for achieving the goal
- to identify means for evaluating progress toward and actual achievement of the goal
- to set measureable and/or performance objectives for each of the next three academic years
- to select and schedule means for achieving 1976-77 objectives

Each task force will receive a typed copy of all pertinent suggestions and comments made by Round Three respondents.

Membership on each task force will be of three kinds: co-chairperson, core member, or associate member. Core members will be expected to meet regularly and actively contribute to the realization of the tasks listed in the previous paragraph. Associate members will be invited to occasional meetings (perhaps two each semester) to provide input, give reactions, etc. Everyone within the college community is encouraged to join in this effort, with all full-time faculty and administrative staff being expected to affiliate with one of these task forces. Choice of affiliation should be based upon the area of greatest interest to you, and the extent to which you are willing to expend your time and energies helping the Mount achieve a particular goal. One co-chairperson will be selected from an area closely related to the goal; the other from the college community at large.

Task Force membership will be based upon your willingness to serve, as indicated on the preference forms at the end of this report. Your completed form may be returned to me in care of Box 72 on the Chalon campus, or the box provided for this purpose in the foyer of Building 7 on the Doheny campus. Sister Mary, Sister Catherine Therese, and I, as facilitators of the RAMP project, will organize and announce the Task Force memberships in February. Toward this end, may we ask you, please, to give thoughtful consideration to how you can best help shape what Mount St. Mary's College will be in 1980: and to return your preference form by <u>Friday, January 30</u>.*

As we move into the next phase of our Resource Allocation Management Program, I want both to thank you for your cooperation in the Goals Study, and to share with you the following:

"Sometimes institutions are simply the sum of the historical accident that happened to them; like the sands in the desert they are shaped by influences but not by purposes. Men and women can shape

p. 3

their institutions to suit their purposes provided that they are not too gravely afflicted with the diseases of which institutions die--among them: complaisance, myopia, and unwillingness to choose."

John Gardner

- -

TASK FORCE Preference Form

Please indicate your first, second and third choices of affiliation, plus the kind of contribution you feel you could make (co-chairperson, core member, or associate member):

	Choice	Kind of affiliation
GOAL 1	__________	__________
GOAL 2	__________	__________
GOAL 3	__________	__________
GOAL 4	__________	__________
GOAL 5	__________	__________
GOAL 6	__________	__________

Date________________ Signature________________________

Return this form to Barbara Becker, in care of Box 72 on the Chalon campus, or the box provided for this purpose in the foyer of Bldg. 7 on the Doheny campus. (Deadline: Friday, January 30, 1976)*

*If you have been away from the college during January and could not, therefore, meet the 30th deadline, please return your preference form to me as soon as possible, no later than Feb. 16.

Thank you!

The first survey instrument circulated among the members of the Community Council had items such as these among the inventory of 53 goals:

> Santa Clara should:
>
> 19. . .identify an experimental college, operated by an elected board, within the financial constraints the enrollment suggests. This unit would be free for total experimentation, and could be a source of curricula innovation and relevance to today's student interests.
>
> 20. . .seek year-round operation by initially subsidizing a summer quarter which would seek national enrollments. It would be a major financial bonanza to Santa Clara to provide more summer income.
>
> 21. . .use its scholarship funds to attract students who have won California state scholarships, and not support those who did not. This is the caliber of students Santa Clara seeks, and this is the best use of limited resources.
>
> 22. . .establish some "pinnacles of excellence", singling out for additional support some departments which have already gained momentum. The University lacks the resources to advance on a broad front. Visibility in selected areas will provide a "halo" effect for the entire institution.

Respondents simply rated each item on a five-point scale from very important to not important.

Robert Pardon, in a follow-up article three years later (1975), still expressed faith in the value of using the Delphi Technique to obtain consensus, but warned against thinking that use of the Delphi Technique would endow the planning effort with the ability to mandate implementation. He said:

> In this connection, it is well to remember the effective uses that can be made of councils and committees. They can review co-ordination; they are less effective for implementing a specific program. Specific programs are best implemented by a person who is given that authority and responsibility. The enthusiasm for the Delphi Technique, for identifying consensus, must

> therefore not be confused with the leadership, inspiration, motivation, and drive that are necessary for goal attainment. This is perhaps more critical in the academic environment than in the military or business activity. (Page 342)

We shall conclude our discussion of leadership in the final chapter; but for now—just to reinforce Pardon's observation—remember that planning without presidential leadership is a rudder without a ship. Also remember that the Delphi Technique was designed for use by experts—that is, to obtain the views of experts. It often goes wrong when used to tap the views of the uninformed.

TWO CASE EXAMPLES OF ORGANIZED LONG-RANGE PLANNING

The University of Washington (Seattle)

The University of Washington is one of the nation's largest and most comprehensive research universities, having the largest single-campus enrollment west of Minnesota and Texas. About a third of the state's bachelor's, half of the masters, over two thirds of the doctorate, and nearly 90% of the first professional degrees are conferred by the University annually. In recent years it has consistently ranked in the top three among all universities in the amount of federal grant and contract awards, and, despite its distance from Washington DC, it ranks among the top ten universities in the number of faculty members who are serving on advisory committees to the Federal Government.

In 1972, with the Regents' approval of A Planning Outline for the University of Washington, the University began its first full-scale planning process, which led in 1974 to the approval of the first Proposed Six-Year Plan (1975-1981). Two years were invested in that proposed plan, yet it has scarcely been referred to since its distribution in January 1975. While the plan was decentralized, as I recommend, so that each school and college—indeed, each department—developed its own plan, there were at least two major difficulties. First, the recommended criteria for assessing school, college, and department plans were not exacting enough. See the list in Figure O. For example, there was no requirement to present a unified strategy with operational substance that clearly built on the unit's salient strengths, was linked to emerging opportunities, or suggested that the plan might be sufficiently stimulating to encourage good minds.

As one who participated in this exercise, I knew each unit simply composed a "wish list" made up of the individual expectations of the

Figure O

CRITERIA SUGGESTED FOR A UNIVERSITY'S PLAN*

a. The need or demand for unit programs as indicated by student interest, opportunities for employment or graduate study, needs for research or service programs, and others.

b. Unit impact and benefits - The impact and benefits of the unit's programs within both academic and non-academic community.

c. Unit quality levels that enable graduates to meet academic or professional objectives or as evaluated by institutional peer rankings, surveys of graduates, provision of external funding, or other means.

d. Unit scale sufficient to enable efficient and effective operations as evaluated by numbers of faculty representing key specializations, total research funding or other measures.

e. Unit productivity as indicated by numbers of graduates and rates of student progress to completion, scholarly and artistic activity, the volume of service activities, or other such indicators.

f. Costs of unit programs evaluated in terms of program results or benefits, the cost of comparable programs in the University or elsewhere, and other costs.

g. The availability and quality of faculty support for the programs as indicated by participation in the instruction, research, or other academic activities involved.

h. Consideration and evaluation of success by students and other parties or clients involved in or influenced by unit programs.

i. Maturity of unit programs at this institution: new, expanding, stable, etc.

j. The advantages of offering the programs at the University. This includes consideration of comparable programs conducted elsewhere showing why the specific capabilities of this institution or the unit make it a better source of the educational or other services provided. Some of the factors to be considered include efficiencies through unique or shared resources, the existence of joint benefits of the program—to both graduate and undergraduate programs—or particular characteristics of the local, regional and national environments.

*From Planning Guide for the years 1974-1981, University of Washington, 1973, pp. 23-24.

faculty members. There was no serious review of the unit's plan using the suggested criteria.

A second weakness was the failure to link the "wish list" directly to the next biennial budget request. The result was to ignore the "plan", even if it had some long-term strategic substance, in order to concentrate on the amount of money the unit will get over the next two years. The integration of the results of this planning exercise into the University's operations was overseen by the University Budget Committee. I don't believe any unit saw the planning process as anything other than a necessary evil to obtain money for next year.

Aside from separating the planning process from so obvious a link to the budget, I would have recommended other criteria to supplement or even replace the ten general criteria I suggest colleges use. (See the following chapter.)

The plan would have a greater chance of success if, in addition to criteria already suggested elsewhere, as many of the following criteria as possible were met satisfactorily:

> The proposed plan (1) recognizes the metropolitan (Seattle) location of the University; (2) builds on the particular interests and resources of the Pacific Northwest; (3) takes special advantage of the strengths of related fields; (4) would be certain to retain as well as attract distinguished faculty members, and so on.

Furthermore, if the central administration, in consultation with leaders among the faculty as well as community-political leaders, thought the following were important, they too would be applied as criteria for testing the "goodness" of plans developed in the constituent units:

> The proposed plan (1) encourages cross-disciplinary research, teaching, and service. (2) ensures expanding opportunities for those who may have been discriminated against because of sex, age, race, or creed. (3) extends services to the community.

The point is that unless specific and relevant qualitative criteria are rigorously applied to proposed strategic directions, the planning process will simply be a waste of time. The criteria presented in the next chapter serves as a general set of guidelines for all colleges and universities; but it is useful, as demonstrated above, to supplement them (or replace them) to suit a particular location, time, or institutional preference as determined by that institution's leadership.

Even as I write this, partly in recognition of the last failure in planning, the University is engaged in another effort. This time it is a ten-year plan. Unfortunately, it is again largely a compendium of resource wants, with insufficient attention to programmatic direction. Perhaps worst of all, the time for "planning" was burlesque. Quite literally, the participants in the academic program I take part in were asked on a Tuesday morning if we could have our ten-year plan ready by Friday, presumably by late Friday afternoon.

The College of St. Benedict

St. Benedict is a Catholic Benedictine women's college located about 80 miles northwest of Minneapolis in the small town of St. Joseph. Enrollment is about 1500, nearly all in residence on campus. Nearby are St. John's University, a men's Catholic institution, and Saint Cloud State University.

The College has had eight years of continuous comprehensive planning experience, which is overseen by the Planning Committee, consisting of all the chief administrative staff members (including the president) along with two faculty members, one student, and one trustee. The Planning Committee sees its primary responsibility as that of a managing group. ". . .the Planning Committee manages the planning process. It involves other groups who have the responsibility for developing strategies through which new goals and objectives are to be achieved." (Escher, 1976, Page 10). The "other groups" are task teams with chairpersons from the Planning Committee. A third planning level is established through Unit Study Committees which are responsible to the Task Teams. Each spring the Planning Committee reviews its priorities and establishes task teams for next year's emphases.

A mobile (Figure P) illustrates the Planning Committee's concept of the continuous planning "structure". The ovals represent non-static groups, hanging by strings, joined by curved supension lines, assuring flexibility. "The mobile has the quality of movement, of changeability, thus further emphasizing the planning process as subject to change when the 'breeze' so indicates." (Escher, 1976, Page 13)

One of the most important annual activities of the Planning Committee is to re-evaluate the position of the College as changes occur in its

Figure P

PLANNING MOBILE FOR A COLLEGE*

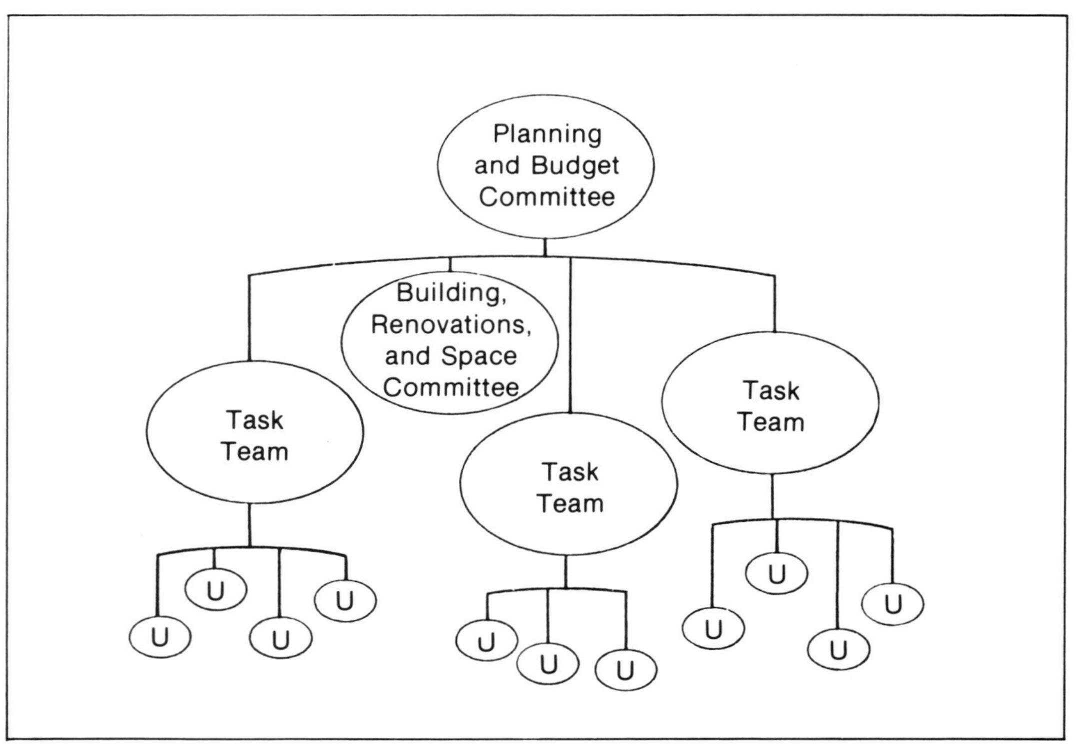

*From Escher, 1976.

environments (economic, social, cultural). Therefore an extensive list of assumptions is re-examined and revised as necessary each year. From a 1976 report, I note these assumptions among 81 others:

1. The tuition gap between private and public institutions will widen.

2. The number of students in the 18-to-22 age bracket in four-year liberal-arts colleges will decrease in the 1980s. Competition for students will be keener.

3. The society will continue to seek purposeful leisure.

4. Stopping out and transferring will be more common.

5. Urbanization will continue.

6. The interdependence of St. John's University and the College of St. Benedict will remain necessary and desirable.

The assumptions, instead of using the four-sided framework suggested in Chapter 4 (Economic, Political, Social, Technological), are grouped by descending environmental impact on the college from national level through state level to college level. Although these assumptions have not been treated this way, it would be feasible to take each assumption and trace its probable impact on the College as illustrated in Figure Q.

In addition to a fixed calendar for annual activities (review and revise national, state, and institutional assumptions, October 1st; review task team reports, March 15th), the Planning Committee has a clear plan for processing its work, as illustrated in Figure R.

The primary benefit of having the planning organized as it is at the College is the consistent way the College can examine its actions in relation to systematic environmental scanning. Continuous adaptation is enhanced.

The President is also directly involved, and as I suggest in Chapter 6, the president, as "architect of strategy", plays a key role.

Even the link to budget recommending (another task of the Planning Committee) is not the serious drawback here that I feel it was at the University of Washington, since this committee's work is ongoing, and the recommendations on budget matters occur many months after the plans are proposed and reviewed.

Figure Q

NATIONAL/STATE/COLLEGE LEVEL ASSUMPTIONS

Impact \ Assumptions	National	State	College
Economic	Tuition levels at private will increase faster than at public colleges, etc.	Same as national	Approximately 6 percent increase is anticipated annually
Political	Federal government will continue to foster programs aiding the private sector, etc.	No additional support anticipated	More emphasis is to be placed on contacts in Wash.
Social	Strong push for women's rights will continue for another 4-6 years	Relative less activity within the state	CSB will gain by being a college for today's woman
Cultural	Increasing proportion of students will come from a drug-using culture, etc.	Same as national	Students traditionally served by CSB will be less influenced than the national and state averages

FLOW CHART FOR PLANNING ISSUES

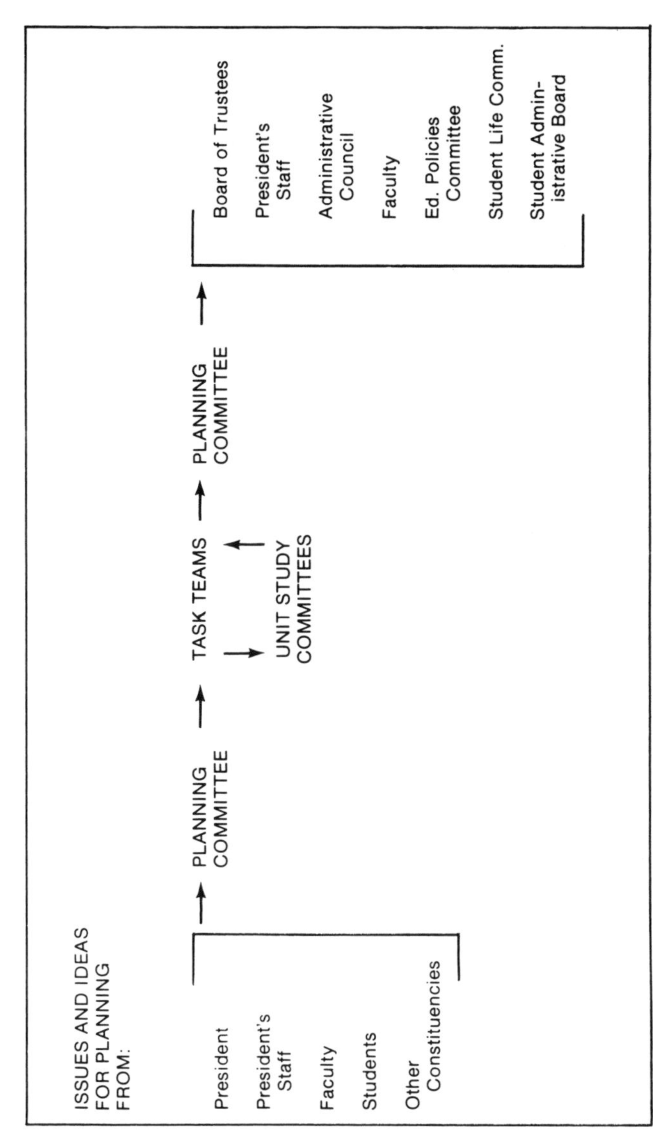

*From Escher, 1976.

A TEN-STEP STRATEGIC PLANNING PROCESS

Since my emphasis throughout this book has been on the creative, imaginative, intuitive plan, it may seem incongruous to now present a ten-step, how-to-do-it "formula" for strategic policy planning. This is done simply to suggest a general path: one which can be departed from given the particular circumstances at any institution, but one which if followed can make certain that trustees, presidents, and faculty members will be faced with an awareness of the consequences of decisions before they are made instead of afterward. Thus the planning process described on these pages is intended as a general, yet practical, and systematic guide to those charged with leading a planning effort.

The recommended steps (largely in outline form) are synthesized from my experience and referenced to practices at some of the institutions used as examples in this chapter. Ideas presented on the planning literature, as well as examples of the application of certain concepts that are now popular in the current literature, such as open systems analysis, MBO, and PPBS, also are used as benchmarks.

Before getting to the ten-step process, a few general observations are in order. First, there will be problems. No strategic planning process will be as easy in practice as the examples in this chapter suggest. Many staff members are going to resist planning generally and the data needed for planning for a number of reasons, including the following:

1. Any examination of current institutional operations is likely to generate tension among those responsible by implying that there is some dissatisfaction with present operations and that changes are imminent.

2. Effective plans must be specific about goals and assumptions, and therefore those whose goals and assumptions are not consistent with the stated planning objectives will be placed in a controversial position.

3. Administrators in particular may see any statement of plans as a potential source of limitations on their operations. For example expediency and "seat-of-the-pants" decisions can be more easily examined in relation to stated policies.

4. Idealists and realists will come into conflict over statements about assumptions and goals.

5. Some staff members will object to any statement of plans on the ground that it is simply impossible to plan in a turbulent environment.

6. Some staff members will not be interested in the planning process because there is no immediate payoff.

These points about human problems are made because it has been obvious to me that many well-intended but unsuccessful attempts have been made at planning in the past. Some planning efforts have failed because those responsible were not conversant with an adequate planning methodology. Failure more often results, however, from some of the personal and political problems mentioned above.

Dealing with these problems is not easy, and no easy solution is suggested. Nevertheless, the problems can probably be minimized if a systematic decision-making procedure is followed, and if both faculty members and administrators anticipate the realities of these problems.

Who should get involved? Nearly all effective planning efforts have required a central planning team serving in a policy-recommending and responsibility-allocating capacity. The team should be a primary responsibility of the president's office, for there rests the greatest prestige as well as the institution-wide perspective necessary for successful planning. A common mistake has been to assign too many individuals to the central planning team in order to satisfy the interests of many groups. A group of seven to nine should be large enough to provide sufficient perspective and small enough to be workable. Without widespread participation, however, the planning function is committed to oblivion. Goal inventories, Delphi Techniques, hearings, calls for submissions, and the establishment of working groups will provide for ample participation.

Working groups in particular should be established first primarily for providing information, and later primarily for advising the central planning team. An office of institutional research or a planning and budgeting office can provide staff assistance and data. To provide adequate horizontal and vertical communication, each task group should be "linked" to the central planning committee and to one or more of the other task groups in the fashion illustrated in Figure S. Task groups should continually change depending on assignments.

Ideally, the process of planning should be directed by an individual who is thoroughly familiar with planning techniques and who has no direct personal interest in their outcome. The director is the key person providing leadership. A certain rigor is required in the process, and this person must insist on "vertical" thinking between steps but "lateral" thinking (de Bono, 1975) within each step.

Figure S

LINKING PLANNING GROUPS

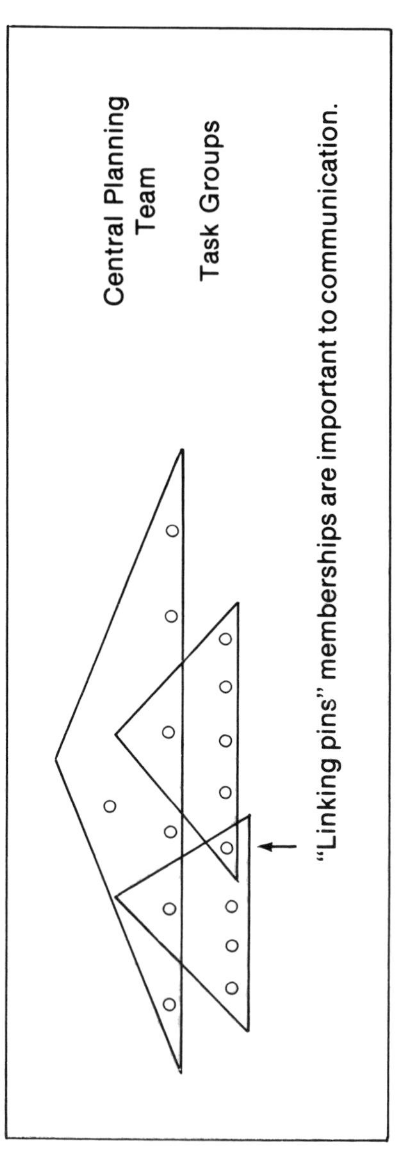

"Linking pins" memberships are important to communication.

When and How Long to Plan. Since it appears that few institutions actually do any systematic planning (Richardson et al., 1977), most institutions would profit from applying systematic methods to the evaluation of their current functioning and future plans as soon as possible. Before implementation, the development of strategic plans should probably take at least a year and a half for most smaller, single purpose-institutions, and several years for most complex universities. Given the variety of functions and areas encompassed by most colleges, the overall planning effort, even under the best circumstances, will probably require at least two years—a relatively short time to invest in the establishment or confirmation of goals likely to be influential for decades.

How to Plan. The remainder of this chapter is devoted to a suggested process for planning which identifies on a step-by-step basis the inherent logic of starting with a statement of an institution's purpose (mission, philosophy, intentions) and continues through a series of decision-making points to a finished strategic plan with operational specifics as well as review procedures. This process is illustrated in Figure T.

The Strategic Planning Process

Effective planning must be more than a casual week-to-week or weekend activity. In addition to the director, several other staff members should be free from the distractions of regular responsibilities so that their full effort can be devoted to this task. Rotating faculty members as full-time planning "consultants" might be possible.

Planners should be provided with a physical setting that includes working space solely for the staff as well as space for the library of resource materials that will surely accumulate. A "Weyerhaeuser Strategic Analysis" room can be developed at little cost.

The director of the planning process must be aware that confusion over the process used in making choices may be as bad as a poor process, and that therefore the process of decision making should be orderly and follow a carefully developed agenda. The steps recommended for this process are presented next, with brief comments on rationale and some examples to give concreteness.

The examples are only suggestive of what should be accomplished to fulfill the requirements of a particular step in the process. Every institution has its unique characteristics, and thus these examples will not be appropriate to all institutions.

Figure T

OVERALL PLANNING SCHEMATIC

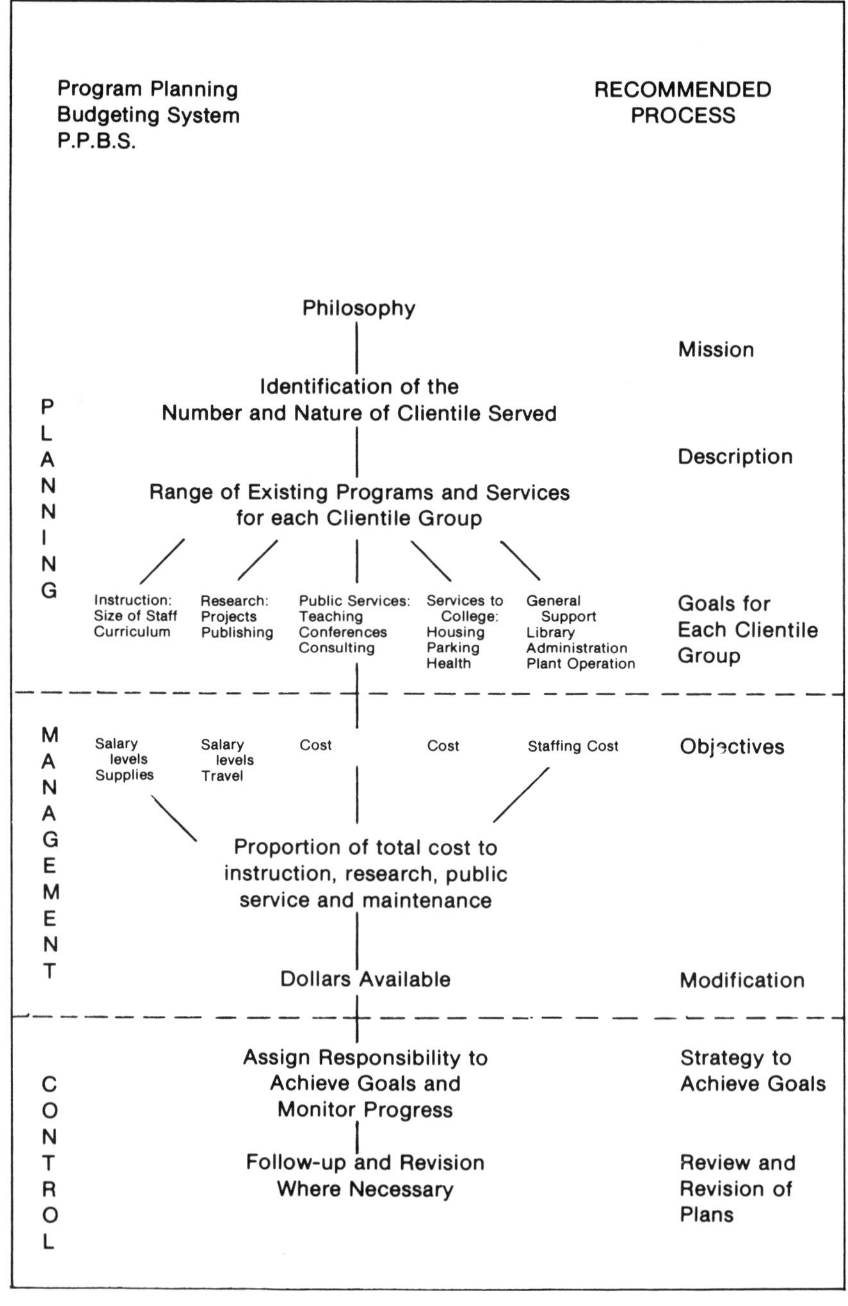

Figure T illustrates the general conceptual schemes associated with the now passe PPBS (left column), the usual—if unstated—way higher educational institutions process annual activities (center), and (in outline) the process described here for developing strategic policies (right).

While I recommend that the process result in a set of stated policies adopted as appropriate and communicated throughout the institution, I am also aware that because of fierce competition between institutions, there are times when it is not desirable to make announcements. I am thinking, for example, of an urban institution that intends for the first time to move programs into suburban locations, directly competing in some instances with other institutions, and in other instances at other locations, noting voids in higher-educational offerings that it can fill.

> *Establishing the missions and goals of the institution is the first step toward the effective use of resources. As a next step, every college should develop a strategy that will successfully guide the institution toward those goals.*
>
> *—From the Management and Financing of Colleges, Committee for Economic Development, 1973*

Step 1. Re-Examine an Existing Statement or Make an Initial (Tentative) Statement of the Institution's Purpose.

This statement of purpose or philosophy provides a foundation, a sense of direction, a single overriding purpose, which serves as the fundamental justification for the institution's existence.

See the catalogues of relatively-unique institutions such as Reed, Goddard, or Evergreeen State College. The following is a reasonably-concrete example from the College of St. Benedict:

> The Mission of the College
>
> No other work of the Planning Committee is more important than reviewing our mission statement, continuously studying it to keep the reality of our purpose before us and to relate our goals to it. In the first year of serious planning, the Master Planning Committee indicated that "the college has a strong sense of mission; that it has a particular identity; that its

> message must be articulated and transmitted; that it has ideals to share and preserve."
>
> We believe that the College of Saint Benedict should remain small, that it should be specifically Catholic, Christian, and Benedictine.
>
> We believe that the communal, shared, residential aspect of our life outside the classroom is important enough to be identified and preserved.
>
> We believe that total human growth is our educational goal; intellectual and emotional, cognitive and affective, contemplative and active qualities are to be represented and honored in the lives of the faculty and students.
>
> We believe that a life of free and daring service may be the chief fulfillment we hope for our students (Directions for the Future, Volume 3, Page 26, 1973).

Most institutions have mission statements. In that case, it is merely important for the planning team to re-examine the statement. Later in the recommended process, the statement of mission will be examined again, this time more carefully.

Step 2. Engage in a Futures Search, Followed by the Formulation of a List of Key Assumptions.

Every conference or workshop conducted by the Centre for Continuing Education at the Australian National University (ANU) begins with a searching look into the future—both the future in general and the specific economic, social, technical, and political factors of strategic significance to the client. Just as the airline industry must anticipate changing points of departure and arrival of passengers many years into the future (airplanes may be delivered from two to eight years after being ordered) and the communications industry must anticipate technological advances, so too colleges and universities need to have some ideas about the changes likely to occur.

One approach is the futures search practiced at the ANU. The essential idea is to anticipate what things people will value, then work back to the impact of what they will value on the programs offered by the institution. The value system outlined in Figure C identifies some dimensions of shifting values. Other "things" that might be valued by next generations could include more emphasis on social skills; work as a service to the common need rather than as a life pursuit to "line the pocket"; education for a full life, for self-actualization, for self-expression, as an expression of joy, and so on.

Faculty groups can be involved in futures searches as well. One approach would be to ask the economics faculty to come up with a scenario of what will happen in their domain, particularly in the critical areas touching on the institution - such as a changing pattern of employment in the area served. The political-science faculty, the sociologists, and other faculty groups might be invited to do the same. These scenarios can be circulated among groups for critiques to come up with a most-likely scenario. From these scenarios it is desirable to identify "optimistic", "pessimistic", and "most probable" outcomes, particularly on those variables of strategic significance to the institution.

Another way of eliciting futures thinking would be to have the planning committee examine the writings of "futurists" such as Kenneth Boulding, Rollo May, Margaret Mead, Herman Kahn, and E. F. Schumacher.[4]

The point of doing futures search is to disconnect the participants from what they already know so well so that a new range of variable perspectives can be brought to bear on the task of planning.

Conclude the futures search by constructing an initial, tentative list of assumptions. Figure Q may be helpful for organizing assumptions, or simply start a list and organize them later. Examples of tentative assumptions are:

1. Improved high-school programs will eliminate the need for certain learning experiences to be provided by the college.

2. The population of youth coming from farm homes or agricultural communities will decline significantly.

3. The number of jobs in the area will decline significantly for the foreseeable future, suggesting the need to educate youth for employment in other communities.

[4]A useful reference would be Michael Marien's critical guide to the futures literature, Societal Directions and Alternatives, Lafayette, New York: Information for Policy Design. Another possibility is Willis Harman's An Incomplete Guide to the Future, San Francisco Book Company, 1976. There are now new views on the future every month. Consult one of your campus's futurists.

4. There will be a shift toward cultural inclusion of the aged linked to lengthening life span, earlier retirement, and better health among the elderly.

5. Institutional boundaries will become less important as institutions become more tightly interconnected.

6. Chronic unemployment and under-employment will continue, perhaps becoming worse over the years.

Step 3. Desribe the Institution and Its Service Area or Zones of Commitment.

The college must know where it is and what it is, at least in the following six quantitative areas, which are for the most part easily summarized from HEGIS and similar reports. The registrar and Office of Institutional Research will have most of the information. If they have little useful data, it may be important to strengthen the institution's data base as an important part of the strategic plan that is developed.

1. Instruction

Input: Number and types of clients (students, adults, etc.) served, where, quality indices, and so on

Process: Distribution of enrollments by department and division

Calculation of average class sizes by department and level of instruction

Cost of instruction

Calculation of instructional loads per faculty

Use of facilities, including an inventory of facilities

Output: Dropout, stopout, and transfer data

Degrees granted by major

Where the students have gone

Academic achievement

2. Research

Input: Number of projects, type, number of proposals submitted, dollar volume

Process: Growth of research facilities

Type of research: basic, applied, developmental

Number of research faculty members

Proportion of time devoted to research, writing, artistic activities

Output: Articles and books published, artistic presentations, research reports, papers read

3. Services to the public

Teaching of non-credit courses, workshops, conferences

Consulting: Including membership with community and professional groups

Regulation and inspection: For example, agricultural stations

Service: For example, sharing computer systems

Facilities: For example, providing housing for community-oriented programs

4. Services to the college clientele

Financial Aid: Students served, levels of support, number of staff members providing service

Care and Recreation:

Housing for students

Food service

Book store

Health service

Parking

Cultural activities

Student organization and activities

5. General support

Learning Resources: For example, library and television

Plant operation and maintenance

Administration (central)

Alumni Association

6. Characteristics of the District or Region Served

Population studies (how many? where?)

Socio-economic characteristics (income, employment, and the like)

Industrial and agricultural enterprises

Transportation network

Communication network

Enrolllment patterns

Step 4. Identify Major Strengths.

The strengths of the institution and the assets in the community which provide a definite advantage in carrying out its mission should be clearly identified, because they often offer an opportunity for service beyond current levels or quality improvements without high additional costs. Examples of assets are:

1. Excellent road and public transportation networks throughout the service area

2. Faculty members with specialized skills in certain areas

3. Favorable relations with neighboring institutions; many co-operative educational programs

4. Under-utilized hours in the late afternoon and evening

5. Highly-ranked, nationally-visible departments

Questions about strengths and weaknesses generally focus on six types of resources:

1. Technical: What is the current state of technological expertise and research capability? How does the institution compare to other institutions with similar objectives?

2. Physical: What is the present condition of plant and equipment? How flexible are they? Is potential capacity being utilized?

3. Financial: What is the present financial condition? Tuition? Endowments? Extra Properties?

4. Human: Does the institution have the academic strength needed in all areas? Are management (governance) skills available?

5. Location: How well is the institution served by transportation networks? What population centers are nearby?

6. Image: How is the institution perceived by potential clients, government officials, donors, neighboring institutions?

Step 5. Identify Major Weaknesses.

Identifying weaknesses and strengths is perhaps the simplest way to describe the college, and provides a setting in which to begin systematically looking ahead. The steps in this process are therefore transitional: past to future. Examples of weaknesses might include geographical isolation, unevenness in the quality of faculty members, distance from the population center of the region, disinterested trustees, too small size to offer a variety of specialized educational programs, and so on.

One of the major challenges to planning, especially that part of planning related to prioritizing, is how to identify a weakness or a strength. Frankly, there isn't a good answer. We do, however, have the experience of the New York system, which has the dubious distinction of going through more retrenchment than other state system. This process has resulted in the development of quality (strong/weak), need (high/low), and cost (good/poor) criteria that can serve as basic measures in this planning process. The best source of information on the "New York System" is forthcoming in an article by Robert Shirley and J. Fredericks Volkwein, both of SUNY-Albany, in the Journal of Higher Education. The essence of the approach the article describes more fully is in lists of (1) evaluative criteria and (2) related rating categories. Those criteria and categories are as illustrated below. I recommend them to you as a starting point from which to develop criteria more appropriate to other campuses or systems.

Evaluative Criteria	Rating Categories
Quality:	
Quality of Faculty	Exceptional, Strong, Adequate, Weak
Quality of Students	High, Medium, Low
Quality of Library Holdings	Excellent, Adequate, Insufficient
Quality of Facilities and Equipment	Excellent, Adequate, Insufficient
Need:	
Centrality to Mission	Yes, No
Present Student Demand	High, Moderate, Low
Projected Student Demand	Growing, Stable, Declining
Demand for Graduates	High, Medium, Low
Locational Advantage	Yes, No
Comparative Advantage	Yes, No
Cost:	
Cost/Revenue Relationship	Good, Adequate, Poor

Step 6. Again Identify Assumptions, Particularly About the Future.

The value of much of the preceding process is likely to become apparent as the planning team now has a common base of reference from which to view the future. The setting down of assumptions is more than merely an exercise; this step should bring out underlying assumptions some members of the group have been carrying which are not shared by others. Unless there is a clear view of these basic assumptions before goal setting the process may flounder. Examples of such assumptions are:

1. Non-book or periodical media will become substantially more important within the next ten years.
2. Inflation will average 10% per year.
3. The population in the service area will decline.
4. The University's fiscal autonomy will continue to be respected.
5. There will be no major state-wide realignment or consolidation of the public segments of higher education during the planned-for period.
6. There will be increased demand for professional and career-oriented programs both on and off the campus.
7. Continuing education for physicians and allied health professionals will continue to expand.

Step 7. Make a New Statement About Mission (Revised as Necessary) and Identify Goals (Broad Aims, Ends).
This is where statements are made describing the institution as it ought to be. Where does the institution wish to go?

Even at this stage of planning it is easy to confuse strategic policy planning and tactical planning. Indeed, the differences are often simply matters of degree. There are, however, three basic differences: (1) strategic planning is not short-term; (2) strategic planning involves the total entity, not just disjointed parts or departments; and (3) strategic planning tends to be oriented toward certain ends, not toward the means of accomplishing them.

While it may seem that the planning process should start with a discussion and setting of goals, it is strongly recommended that any consideration of goals be delayed until a background for realistic goal setting has been established. Unless the central planning group are deliberately delayed, they will likely find themselves (1) considering too limited or too grand a range of possibilities, because they do not know themselves or the institution well enough, and (2) confused with regard to a necessary separation of means and ends.

The next step in the planning process is one in which more attention is paid to the means of achieving goals. Here the realists have their day. Here is where balance is assured. Feasibility looms large. As Majone (1975) puts it so well:

> ...feasibility, rather than optimality, is a realistic goal for the policy analysis. Feasibility should be defined in terms of all the relevant constraints: social, political, administrative, and institutional, as well as technical and economic. When all these

> constraints are taken into consideration, the range of feasible choices turns out to be much more restricted than is usually assumed... Some constraints...result from prior decisions or conventions...new constraints are very often discovered in the process of implementation. Policy failures, and the appearance of unanticipated consequences, are telling signs that important constraints have been disregarded at the moment of decision, or that the boundary conditions are changing. (Page 65)

Step 8. Determine Guiding Objectives (Means, Milestones).

The objectives are specifics achievable at definite points in time (short-range or long-range). Like mission and goals, objectives provide a guide to decision making. But more important, as a step in the process, they provide a basis for the data collection and analysis on which the college relies to monitor its progress. In addition, objectives aid in working out the details of the plan, such as assigning responsibilities to departments. At this stage in the process, keep the objectives tentative. Examples of such objectives are:

1. Achieve year-round operation, with balanced enrollments each term, in three years.

2. Enroll 15% of the student body from minority groups by 1980.

3. Reduce the proportion of X to X% of the student body by 1985.

4. Reduce the frequency with which courses enrolling fewer than ten students are offered.

5. Increase scholarship support by an average of 10% annually.

6. Increase service to the unemployed and welfare recipients 20% annually for five years.

7. Double the number of co-operative programs with industry by 1985.

8. Phase out X program by 1985.

For an excellent guide for writing objectives, see James Harvey's Managing Colleges and Universities by Objectives (1976), pages 56-60.

Analysis of the Objectives

An analysis of past trends and a projection into the future becomes especially important at this stage of the planning process, because we are examining the potential of achieving the goals and objectives. At this stage planning gaps are uncovered: the differences between desired objectives that can be quantified and trend forecasts.

An analysis of past trends is desirable because these trends identify the base lines of the institution's natural momentum. The basic assumption the planning groups must consider is that the trends will continue unless through this planning process specific changes are sought or are bought upon the institution because environmental forces change.

Thus trend data, where quantifiable, should be presented in the form of percentages and ratios if possible, because they more accurately reflect interaction among components of the institution and the environment. Ratios, furthermore, are easier to analyze than raw data. For example see Figure U.

Because of the crucial importance of this step to the remainder of the planning process, the tentative objectives should be worked out with great care and carefully related to strengths and opportunities. It is at this point that the cost of achieving each objective must be identified and the costs of time and funds must be compared with the available staff and financial resources. In all likelihood, the objectives important to achieve certain goals will call for resources of a greater magnitude than are realistically available. "Aspirations budgets" covering five to ten years thus need to be developed for each goal area. It is at this point in the process that modification will be required. See Step 9.

Step 9. Make Additional Modifications of Mission, Goals, and Objectives

Going through this difficult step is necessary to assure some balance between idealism and realism. See Figures V and W. Goals sought can be prioritized by linking them to cells in these matrices. Figure V can be a sorting device that gives strategic alternatives comparative visibility. For example an alternative, say to create satellite learning centers, may be valued by the staff (therefore it is wanted); may have sufficient staff and financial resources (therefore it can be done); may capitalize on an opportunity in the environment (therefore it is a promising prospect); and may not face any restraints, such as an unfavorable law or a competing institution (therefore no blocks are present). A similar matrix is

Figure U

DISPLAY OF TIME-LINKED QUANITATIVE MILESTONES

	1976	1977	1978	1979	1980	1981	1985	1990
Proportion of courses oriented to community service	10%	11%	12%	12%	14%	14%	15%	20%
Tuition increase	10%	10%	7%	6%	5%	3%	----	----
Student-Faculty ratio	20:1	21:1	22:1	24:1	26:1	28:1	30:1	30:1
Retention until degree	30%	32%	33%	35%	37%	40%	45%	50%
Faculty turnover	4%	3%	3%	3%	3%	2%	2%	4%
Proportion of offerings off campus	0%	0%	5%	5%	8%	10%	15%	20%
Proportion of students in technical programs	30%	28%	27%	26%	24%	21%	20%	20%

*A Community college

represented in Figure W. The Number 1 cell would be for ideas having a "positive value" reflecting staff desires and positive "opportunity value" in the environment. In this example, "second priority" new ideas (or existing programs) are those valued by the staff; but it could be argued equally that second priority should be given to external opportunities, even though they might have a lower-valued position internally. Before the sorting takes place, a decision needs to be made on how entrepreneural the institution will be. Responding to opportunity is entrepreneural.

Step 10. Synthesize All That is Known to Come Up With Strategic Alternatives

Test the alternatives using the ten criteria in the next chapter. Determine the strategy to achieve goals and assign responsibility for implementation. This is the most difficult step because, while there is some pleasure in specifying goals, the tough questions are how to synthesize planning the elements and how to determine how the college is going to get there? The planning group must now:

1. identify and emphasize specific programmatic dimensions in order to place resources strategically;
2. assign responsibility to operating components of the college;
3. specify action to be taken;
4. obtain any necessary administrative, trustee, or faculty approval.

The strategic plan of Lesley College, a woman's college in Cambridge, Massachusetts, emphasizing the preparation of teachers and other practitioners who work with children, illustrates well what I mean by identifying specific programmatic dimensions, assigning responsibility, and specifying action. The College's 1978-1983 Goals and Objectives statement announced—among other strategies—(1) the establishment of a new division (a structural change), (2) an increased commitment to the equality of women (an attitudinal emphasis), and (3) a comprehensive advancement program (a support goal). Illustrative portions of that plan are in Figure X.

A Concluding Observation

Finally, while the process as outlined on these pages may seem overly structured, plans that do not develop from a rigorous process, or something similar, are not likely to have a comprehensive frame of reference serving both as a starting point and as a continuing guide. A systematic process has the potential of increasing the likelihood that the college can explicitly determine its future—and that is what strategic policy planning is all about.

Figure V

INTERNAL/EXTERNAL TASK FORCES

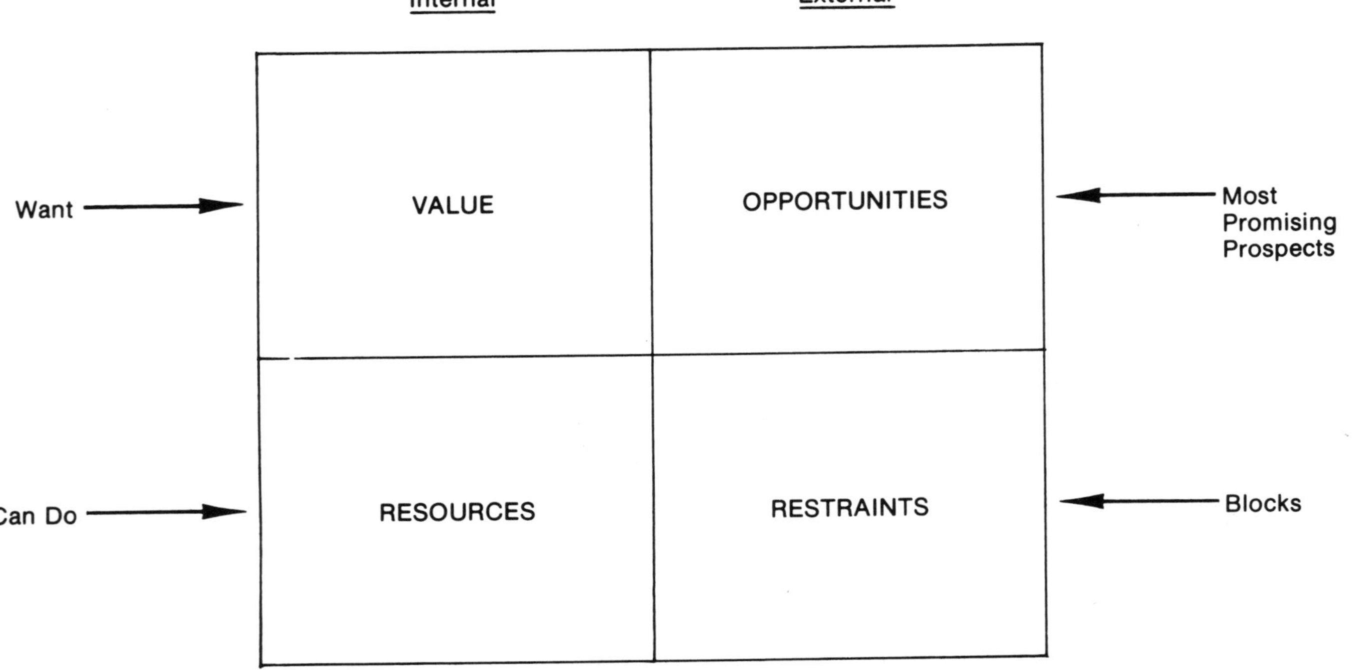

Figure W

PRIORITIZING MATRIX

Environment

(External Opportunities/Values)

Institution (Internal Values)

	+	-
+	GROW (First Priority) 1	PERHAPS MAINTAIN (Second Priority) 2
-	PERHAPS DEVELOP (Third Priority) 3	DON'T CONSIDER OR PHASE OUT (Lowest Priority) 4

Figure X

EXAMPLE FROM A STRATEGIC PLAN*

- 1 -

I. Mission and Means

A. The mission of Lesley College will continue to be the professional preparation of teachers and other practitioners who work with children. Levels of preparation through the doctorate and various specialized programs may be included within this mission, but each will be tested against the college's commitment to professional education.

B. In order to pursue its mission the College will be arranged in three major divisions:

1. The Undergraduate College will remain a small, high quality, independent institution for women. Students will prepare to become elementary school teachers or to enter other careers related to the needs of children. Within this focus the Undergraduate College will be sensitive to new needs and will consider programs to meet them.

2. The Graduate School will continue to emphasize increasing quality in advanced programs for educational professionals, in-service programs for the renewal and growth of teachers, and the professional preparation of liberal arts graduates for entry into teaching. Within these areas the Graduate School will continue to be unusually sensitive to the needs of the field and will maintain its ability to meet professional needs with flexibility and high quality.

3. Lesley College will add a new, third division: the Lesley Collaborative for Educational Development (LCED). This new arm of the institution will not administer degree programs but will work directly with professionals, agencies and institutions in the field.

LCED will assist in innovation, consultation and assessment. It will provide leadership and support to schools which need policy research, to professionals and organizations which seek assessment and self-renewal, and to lay groups such as school boards which seek consultation. It will work with the broad variety of entities which have an educative function in society: business, industry, social agencies, rest homes, hospitals, publishers, half way houses, detention centers, foster homes and prisons.

*From Lesley College, Goals and Objectives, 1978-1983.

- 2 -

In addition to providing these services on a contract basis the LCED will seek Federal and other funds for worthwhile projects in education and will develop and publish educational materials, films and other learning aids such as those represented in the College's Kresge Center collection.

The LCED will utilize, to a considerable degree, the unique combination of talents to be found at the College. It is expected that by the third year of its existence, the collaborative will be able, through excess of revenues over direct costs, to contribute substantially to the resources needed to maintain the college as a whole.

<u>Objectives</u>:

(1) Appoint chief administrator for LCED.

Target date: May 1978
Responsible: President

(2) Begin operations of LCED.

Target date: September 1978
Responsible: Head, LCED
Resources: within regular budgets (providing meaningful incentive margin within three years)

C. All three of Lesley's divisions will turn particular attention to opportunities in three important areas:

1. As part of its strong commitment to the equality of women, Lesley College must provide the opportunity for all of its members to become aware of sexism in society and to help them combat sexual stereotyping in education. This includes increased emphasis on educational leadership roles for women, examination and understanding of changing sex roles, the two career family and other sex related developments in modern society. Students at Lesley should be made constantly aware of the true alternatives open to them, and offered the chance to learn the skills to pursue whatever alternative they desire. Steps will be taken to assure that by 1983 Lesley will be seen to be a model of non-sexist practices.

- 3 -

Objectives:

(1) The College will establish a committee to monitor sexism and sex role stereotyping. The committee will examine all activities on campus and report annually to the Lesley Community and to the President using Title IX guidelines. The report should include both progress and needed improvements.

The committee will be chaired by the Dean of Students and will include the Dean of the Graduate School and the members of the existing Graduate-Undergraduate Liaison Committee.

Target date: February 1978
Responsible: President, Dean of Students
Resources: within regular budgets

(2) The Undergraduate College will continue two or three workshops per year on these issues for faculty and administration, using some workshops for specific course development or improvement.

Target date: continuing
Responsible: Vice President for Undergraduate Programs
Resources: funds for this in the amount of $600 should be included in the appropriate Vice President's budget

(3) The Graduate School should begin holding workshops on these issues for faculty and administration, using some workshops for specific course development or improvement. One should be held by July 1, 1978 and two to three each year thereafter.

Target date: Spring 1978 and continuing
Responsible: Vice President for Graduate Programs
Resources: funds for this in the amount of $600 should be included in the appropriate Vice President's budget

- 4 -

(4) The Undergraduate College and Graduate School will jointly sponsor workshops on these issues for non-exempt staff. The first will be held by July 1, 1978 and thereafter one will be held each year.

Target date: Spring 1978 and continuing
Responsible: Personnel Liaison Officer
Resources: within regular budgets
(Expertise available within the College can be utilized.)

(5) Each undergraduate division and graduate program will examine its own courses with regard to sexism and sex role.

Target date: some changes should be made by July 1, 1978 and annually thereafter
Responsible: Deans and heads of divisions and programs
Resources: within regular budgets

(6) Programs, conferences and special events will be sought for the purpose of enhancing the image of the undergraduate college as a "Women's College."

Target date: continuing
Responsible: Vice President for Public Affairs
Public Relations Department
January Coordinator
Resources: within regular budgets

(7) Hold a workshop on sex role, sexual stereotyping and sexism for freshmen and transfer students.

Target date: beginning spring 1978
Responsible: Dean of Students
Resources: within regular budgets

- 19 -

IV. Funds and Facilites

A. The financial well-being of the College is the overwhelming responsibility of the Trustees. Members of our Governing Boards are the ultimate conservators of Lesley's future, a future which needs to be assured by the shoring up of the institution's financial security by these prestigious and influential groups. The Chairman of the Board and the President must make their first priority the need to increase substantially the Trustees' and corporators' financial support of the College.

Objective:

(1) Mount the comprehensive advancement program required to provide significantly increased capital, annual and deferred support necessary to contribute appropriately to the programmatic growth implicit in the President's Goals for 1982-83.

Target date: chairpeople and committee members responsible for capital and deferred gift programs enlisted by December 31, 1977 with chairman of the annual programs enlisted soon thereafter.
Responsible: Chairman of the Board of Trustees
Resources: within regular budgets

B. By 1982-83 the Annual Fund should be producing one million dollars: $200,000 (plus) for the operation of the Development Office; $300,000 for the debt service on the new Campus; and $500,000 for scholarships and other costs in operating budget, including $100,000 to permit Lesley to continue its emphasis on innovation. This is essential if we are to continue to maintain and increase our institutional margin of excellence.

It is unrealistic for Lesley to rely almost wholly (93 per cent) upon tuition income to operate the College. In addition to a successful Annual Fund, we need to mount a Capital Funds Campaign. The quasi-endowment fund ($600,000) must be substantially increased. And money must be raised for new construction. It is urgent that we renew our programs in deferred giving.

Objectives:

(1) A formal, ongoing annual gifts campaign, consistent with our capital objectives, will be formulated as our capital program gains momentum. The plan should cover the period to 1982-83 and be completed by the time we launch the public phase of the capital campaign.

Target date: Spring 1978
Responsible: members of the Board, the President and the Vice President for Public Affairs
Resources: within regular budgets

(2) Acquire legal support, prepare legal vehicles and launch a deferred giving program aimed at endowment funds.

Target date: second quarter of 1978
Responsible: leadership - the Governing Boards
support - Vice President for Public Affairs

(3) Promote the image of Lesley College. A positive image and strong identity are essential to a climate conductive to fund-raising. A successful audit, resulting in the formulation of a comprehensive action plan, powerfully articulated in a case for ongoing support for the College, is essential to the achievement of our objectives.

Target date: proceeding presently
Responsible: Public Affairs Office (this is the defined first priority for that office)

An Abbreviated Planning Process

Now, however, for those persons or institutions who sense that the recommended ten-step planning process is not for them, I can recommend a simpler approach. Have the central planning group appoint four task groups to work in four areas as illustrated earlier in Figure V. The groups can simply be called Values, Resources, Opportunities, and Restraints. Values and Resources focus on the internal dimensions of the institution: The Values group determines what is desired by the college—what is wanted and what is valued, while the Resources group specializes in what the college can do best—its strengths and its unused potential. Opportunities and Restraints focus on the external environment: The Opportunities group looks into areas not adequately served to determine what the institution could be most successful at undertaking, while the Restraints group surveys the environment for restraining factors to determine what the institution probably cannot do.

Each task group could go through a simplified version of the ten steps, deleting steps as necessary. "Linking pin" members (Figure S) are especially important.

The Central Planning Committee would still synthesize the process to come up with the cornerstones of the institution's strategic plan, perhaps using a prioritizing matrix like that in Figure W, in which ideas or programs are placed in cells according to how highly they are valued internally or what opportunities for their implementation exist externally. Ideas or programs listed in the "grow" cell are highly valued internally and also valued externally. The lower-left cell would identify ideas which are likely candidates for development because there is support for them in the environment, while the upper-right cell would identify ideas which, while valued by the institution, are candidates for maintenance or slow phasing out because of lower acceptance in the environment (for example, languages).

One approach to prioritizing goals is to establish the location of goals—through group consensus—in a matrix such as that illustrated in Figure W, in which programs or goals are placed in cells according to how clearly the environment (political, economic, and so on) offers possible opportunities (high or low value), and according to how much these programs or goals are valued by the institution. The Bendigo Institute of Technology (Australia) has an exceptional collection of minerals and a strong geology faculty; but because these are no longer valued in Australia (which has many collections of minerals and too many geologists), such a program would be listed in Cell 2. A slightly-conservative approach to prioritizing goals would give more emphasis to existing programs than to opportunities in the environment. A growing interest in quality health care with no program at the college would suggest a third-level priority.

An extension of this form of prioritizing is accomplished by expanding the number of cells to nine, introducing "must", "want", and "like" levels of desire for both the institutional values and the environmental values—"must", "want", and "like" being considered Priorities 1, 2, and 3 (highest to lower).

Like the formulation of strategy, the implementation of strategy is composed of sub-activities which if improperly managed can make even the soundest strategic decision ineffective. The performance of tasks needed to implement any policy decision requires information systems, relationships for the co-ordination of subdivided activities, staff members (including faculty members), development programs, incentive systems, controls, and continuous examination of the institution's strategy. The last-mentioned requirement is perhaps the most important, as it provides a strategy for continuous evaluation and change. Thus the analysis of the process of implementation is as important as the analysis used to determine the choice of strategy.

A principle is never useful or living or vital until it is embodied in an action.
—Manly Hall

Questions to Guide Implementation

After strategic priorities are established, the following questions should help the planning group anticipate what internal decisions should be addressed:

1. How will the campus academic enterprise be organized?

2. What existing programs should be continued?

3. What existing programs should be reviewed with the intention of changing their emphasis?

4. What existing programs should be terminated?

5. What new programs should be initiated?

6. How many students should be enrolled in academic degree programs?

7. To what extent should student-admission control mechanisms be used to achieve an intended distribution of students in academic degree programs?

8. What sub-specialization should the curriculum include?

9. How should new faculty postions be allocated?

10. Is the existing distribution of faculty members by teaching and research specialization campatible with anticipated strategic policy emphases?

11. How should funds be allocated to academic units? What allocation-decision criteria should be employed? How should the budget process operate?

12. Planning and decision making for support services are intimately tied to the budget process, yet are often distinct from strategic policy planning because budgetary-allocation decisions for services are made independently of those made for academic units. This should not be so. How will planning for the campus library, central campus computer facilities, admissions and registering offices, student services, institutional research, and the like be articulated into the overall strategic plan?[5]

No matter what process is followed, the result should be examined using the content checklist illustrated next.

[5]These questions are adapted from the dissertation of Larry Jones (1977), 70-72.

CONTENT CHECKLIST

Those institutional plans, whether formally written and approved by the trustees or simply widely understood, with the highest number of attributes identified on the checklist come closest to meeting the requirements for a full strategic plan.

- Institutional Purpose Defined; Raison d'etat .... ☐
- Strategic Position(s) Concerned with Total Institution .... ☐
- Long-Term Perspective; Not less than Five Years .... ☐
- Tested by 10 Criteria of Chapter Five .... ☐
- Specific Goal(s) Identified .... ☐
- Major Activities/Events Supporting Goals Identified .... ☐
- Timetable Established for Sequencing Activities/Events .... ☐
- Procedures Established for Reviewing Timetable's Accomplishments ..... ☐
- Supporting Budgets Identified .... ☐
- Responsible Staff Identified for Each Goal .... ☐
- Plan is Communicated to All Staff .... ☐
- Means for Annual Review Established .... ☐

- Presidential Support Assured .... ☐
- Approved by Trustees .... ☐

Policy making...depends on all who help to formulate the concrete alternatives between which the policymaker must choose; on all who must help to carry it out; on all those whose concurrence is needed, legally or in practice, to put it into effect; and by no means least, on all those who, by giving or withholding their trust, can nurse or kill its chances of success.

—Sir Geoffrey Vickers, 1965

Chapter 5

Today, if you are not confused you are just not thinking clearly.
—Irene Peter

Discovery consists in seeing what everybody else has seen and thinking what nobody else has thought.
—Albert Szent-Gyorgyi

EVALUATING A STRATEGIC PLAN

Discovering a realistic pattern of goals and policies that makes a "good" strategic plan is difficult. How shall an actual or proposed strategy be judged? How do we know that one strategy is bettern than another?

While no infallible indicators are available, there are a number of useful questions that can be asked to assess the "goodness" of any plan. Even if they are not amenable to precise answers, these questions will lead to improved judgements, improved intuitive discrimination. They may be thought of as criteria, and for ease of application may be stated in a questioning format:

1. Is the plan identifiable?

Be certain the plan contains statements with operational substance, such as: The College will continue to emphasize selective recruiting, and therefore a majority of students will be drawn from certain communities (name them), from certain areas (name them: Southeastern Colorado, Northern California...), from certain Christian denominations (name them), and the like. You will know when the statements are definite enough, because they will become contestable. No one is going to contest goals that lead to the "development of an adequate and positive self-concept and a mature personality", as stated in a planning document on my desk at this moment from a small Southern California college. Similar examples are too common in college catalogues and planning documents. Here are more examples of "planning" statements without operational substance:

> "The College's aim is to contribute to the true good of human life and society."

> "...to involve the members of the academic community of the University in the larger processes and movements of society."

> "...to teach all subjects so as to develop the knowledge, abilities, appreciations, and motivations which are liberating for man."

> "The University will concentrate on those educational activities and programs for which it is uniquely qualified." No mention is made anywhere of how it is uniquely qualified.

And from the University of Washington, printed on the first page of the Appendix in its 1974-1981 Planning Guide:

> Purposes of the University of Washington
> The University is a base for the free generation and exploration of ideas and for the preservation of the intellectual and cultural heritage of mankind. It is a resource provided by society for use by individuals in pursuit of the highest scholarly, esthetic, and humane goals to which mankind can aspire. As such it must both attract and cultivate men and women of high capability and must develop their potentialities as human beings. In turn, society can expect to gain from its universities both increasing knowledge and informed, sensitive, vigorous persons prepared to work toward the improvement of man's condition.

Statements of such broad scope, while necessary to instill a sense of essence, commitment, and value, are not adequate for prioritizing resource applications. And too often institutions stop at the point of providing such phrases. Perhaps this is worse than silence, for the illusion of operational commitment is conveyed when none has been made.

Except for Lesley College, I have not found a college or university with a reasonably-comprehensive strategic plan having operational substance. However Berea College, a private liberal-arts college situated in the Appalachian region of Kentucky, comes close. Berea's primary zone of commitment geographically is to high-ability students from Appalachia with limited economic resources. The curriculum is based on the liberal arts explicitly to provide a core for studies in applied fields important to that region: agriculture, business administration, home economics, industrial arts, nursing, teacher education, and so on. Students can, of course, specialize in Appalachian Studies.

Because many of the earliest staff members at Berea came from Oberlin College prior to the Civil War, there has been a proud emphasis on interracial education within a Christian ethic emphasizing, almost passionately, respect for intellectual freedom and other human freedoms.

Another cornerstone of Berea's goal structure is its labor program, in which all students acquire job experience which enables them to earn money, develop skills, and cultivate attitudes useful in any work role. A wide range of jobs are available both at the College and with any of the businesses and farms owned by the College. The aim is to relate the dignity of mental and manual skills. Of course, the work program also keeps the tuition and fees down to probably the lowest of any private college.

Small as it is (accommodating about 1500 students), the college also maintains itself as a major cultural, service, and information center for the region, with a speaker's bureau, an Appalachian Museum, an Appalachian information center, and a library which, although private, seeks to serve the public needs of the region.

As a clear example of specificity, consider this statement on admissions territory recommended in Berea's 1976-1981 long-range plan:

> The Committee recommends that the College should strengthen its admissions effort by increasing the area defined as its territory from 230 to 257 counties in the same eight Southern states. It would accomplish this change by adding fifteen Kentucky counties which border the present territory to the West and North. They are Boyle, Bracken, Clark, Fleming, Green, Jessamine, Marion, Mason, Mercer, Metcalfe, Monroe, Montgomery, Nicholas, Robertson, and Taylor. In addition it recommends the inclusion of twenty-two West Virginia counties excluded from its territory. These counties are Barbour, Braxton, Cabell, Calhoun, Clay, Doddridge, Gilmer, Harrison, Jackson, Kanawha, Lewis, Marion, Mason, Monongalia, Pleasants, Preston, Ritchie, Roane, Taylor, Tyler, Upshur, and Wirt. At the same time the committee suggests that seven counties of Alabama, at the far southwestern boundary of the existing territory, be excluded, and that three Virginia counties, located at the far eastern boundary of the present territory also be excluded. The Alabama counties are Clay, Cleburne, Fayette, Franklin, Marion, Walker, and Winston. The Virginia counties are Greene, Madison, and Rappahannock.
> (This recommendation was accepted by the Board of Trustees in January 1976.)

While it is easy enough to see how a small, independent college such as Lesley or Berea may have an identifiable strategic plan, what about a large, complex, research university with a wide span of clientele, curricular offerings, service areas, and research interests that are simultaneously local, regional national, international, and galactic?

I would argue that the necessarily-decentralized authority structure in large research universities does not lend itself well to a tidy strategic plan for the university. In its simplest terms, the research university is decentralized because so many different schools and divisions are educating students in history, law, painting, theoretical physics, finance, and orthodontics, while spending millions on hundreds of different research projects, as they offer concerts, conferences, public lectures, short courses, and consulting to the public. There is no way—given the present state of the art—that a university plan can satisfactorily account for the differences in mission and outcome of so many distinct entities. They do so many different things.

Instead of a university strategic plan, the time-honored Harvard concept of "every tub on its own bottom" is recommended. Each entity should have its own strategic plan, and that plan should be examined using the ten criteria suggested here.

Harvard is, of course, not alone in having each school manage its own affairs. The practice is, however, too rare. Recognized exceptions are the "responsibility center" system of the University of Pennsylvania, the "reserve school" system of Washington University (St. Louis), and the "management center" concept of Case Western Reserve University.

The pluralistic nature of a complex research university is recognized in decentralized strategic planning providing for a diversity of decision strategies that recognize system relationships internally and externally. Individual schools and entities would not, of course, function in a policy vacuum. The central administration would maintain institutional values, insist on collaboration between units, provide venture capital, and so on; but most of all the central administration would have to maintain a tolerance for ambiguity and be subtle in action.

2. Does the Strategy Build on the Institution's Strengths?

The point is to link the plan to the known strengths of the institution. If departments X, Y, and Z are strong, then.... If the faculty is avowedly conservative, evangelically Christian..., if it is vocationally oriented..., if it is..., then....

Berea College built initially on the strengths of its Oberlin faculty. Later, as its business and agricultural faculties demonstrated strength, Berea expanded on their skills to own and operate businesses and farms and move into agricultural extension.

The College of St. Benedict (St. Joseph, Minnesota), recognizing its strong fine-arts and performing-arts faculty, builds on that resource to become an important cultural center for the region northwest of Minneapolis.

The University of Hartford, building initially on its business and economics faculties (and, or course, on Hartford's insurance complex), established one of the most successful (and high-cost) evening-school programs in the United States.

In the present era of stable enrollments, more institutions might consider further consolidations around strengths. As in poker, bet the strong hands.

3. Does the Plan Build on Opportunities in the Environment?

The designs of future plans are critically dependent on basing institutional development on opportunities, present and foreseeable. What trends in education, in politics, in health care, in public subsidies, in societal values, in employment are linked to the strategy? What is already in the immediate environment to build on? Or, if one is as imaginative as Iowa State University was to host the First International Conference on Iceberg Utilization (October 1977), then the world of knowledge and its utilization is the environment.

Hampshire College builds on the resources of its neighbors: Amherst, the University of Massachusetts, Smith, and Mount Holyoke. The University of Tulsa draws on its immediate environment to emphasize petroleum geology and related disciplines. The University of Rhode Island—having hardly any land environment—has strength in oceanography (even this is in Massachusetts, at Woods Hole). Rice University builds on both the growing commercial strength of Houston and the adjacent NASA Manned Spacecraft Center to emphasize entrepreneurship, combined with strength in physics, chemistry, math, and of course, engineering, almost to the same extent that Knox College almost ignores its immediate environment (Galesburg, Illinois) to concentrate instead on making academic comparisons with Oberlin and Kenyon and even coyly pretentious references to Harvard, calling it the "Knox of the East", while attracting students from the wealthier surburban communities of Chicago only to send them off to Colorado to study geology, Japan to study art, or the ghettos to study sociology.

Rice and Knox, both viable institutions, illustrate the opposite extremes of adapting to opportunities in the local environment and ignoring the local environement—demonstrating, of course over-simply, that individual criteria cannot stand in isolation, and therefore all criteria must be examined in concert.

4. Is the Plan Consistent with the Expectations of the Most Important Constituencies?

It is useful to think of the different constituencies on and off campus as a series of critical interfaces.[1] For the public institutions, especially state universities, state government is critical. Even private institutions are mindful that their not-for-profit status and other important matters are linked to laws. With nearly 50% of high-school graduates going on to college, many voters are concerned about what colleges do. Therefore public and private college resources must always be kept in high priority "state" goals—even if this includes coaches and recruiters who can win football games.

The Federal Government is, of course, important to those institutions that have moved from the periphery to center stage, while local governments—important to every institution—are particularly important to community and municipal colleges.

Professional associations (especially if certification is involved), parents, alumni, and manpower users round out the constituencies that are important most of the time. A strategic plan needs to anticipate the response, either enabling or restraining, from each important constituency. Vanderbilt University, long a part of the conservative South, where proper gentry could send their most intelligent progeny for intellectual and social finishing, has moved uneasily toward the restless contemporary mainstream, attracting students from suburban Chicago and Southern California to learn from and influence those from Montgomery and Ashtabula—a clear if gradual change in constituencies, with attendant problems. The vast majority of institutions, however, apparently change about as much as Yale, Brigham Young, and the University of Arkansas. Therefore new interfaces with changing constituencies are a problem for only a minority of institutions.

Consistency is the hobgoblin
of little minds.
—Emerson

---

[1]I am grateful to Laura Saunders for suggesting the importance of including a careful analysis of constituencies.

5. Is the Plan Consistent with Competencies and Resources?

The availability of both human competencies and fiscal and physical resources must be determined and programmed on a time scale. Launching a new program in particular will involve substantial start-up costs, and it may be necessary for either public or private institutions to draw on investment assets in endowment; or if a fleeting opportunity occurs a public institution might be able to obtain the necessary political support and rapidly come up with resource increments to "seize the time".

Appalachian Berea and its students have little in economic resources, so the extensive work program keeps costs and fees down; the legislatures of New York and Florida made it possible for their institutions to seize the time during a more optimistic recent past; and Antioch drew on both name and Yellow Springs' fiscal resources to launch its round-the-world off-campus programs.

6. Are Major Portions of the Planning Strategy Internally Consistent?

Look for coherence, compatibility, synergy. Few institutions fully realize cross-benefits. For example, an undergraduate recruiting effort linked to a service program and an off-campus graduate center in a particular community will produce all kinds of unexpected cross-benefits. When the University of Massachusetts established a Medical School in Worcester, about midway between its Amherst and Boston campuses, it lost the benefits of location near supporting schools and departments of—among other things—nursing and biochemistry. A particularly-bad decision, yes; but one brought about, as many are, by the need to reach a political compromise.

The California Institute of Technology owes much of its prestigious reputation in science to the coherence and compatibility of programs such as hydraulics, jet propulsion, and aeronautics, just as the University of Michigan gains from the coherence and synergy of strong departments in the social sciences linked to semi-autonomous, high-powered, applied social-science agencies such as the Institute for Social Research. Likewise, the Claremont Graduate School and Graduate Center appears to be happily compatable with five distinctive undergraduate colleges, as they all share the Hannold Library.

The point of this criterion is to emphasize plans maximizing cross-benefits.

7. Is the Strategy Compatible with the Personal Values and Aspirations of the Faculty and Administration?

Unless the plan is compatible, expect mediocre effort, if not outright sabotage. The failure of the Meyerson/Bennis administration at SUNY-Buffalo in the late 1960s can be traced in large measure to the conflict between personal preferences and goals of the continuing members of the university and those of the new guard. The calamity at Bennington in the mid-1970s was in large measure the result of mis-matched values and aspirations. Lack of fit is a sure harbinger of mediocre effort and probable failure—perhaps even catastrophe.

> *Policy making...depends on all who help to formulate the concrete alternatives between which the policy maker must choose; on all who must help to carry it out; on all those whose concurrence is needed, legally or in practice, to put it into effect; and by no means least, on all those who, by giving or withholding their trust, can nurse or kill its chances of success.*
>
> *—Sir Geoffrey Vickers, 1965*

8. Is the Strategy Consistent with Ethical Values? Is it Socially Responsible?

Although it can be argued that filling any apparent need for an educational service contributes to the social good, it is certainly worth questioning the appropriateness of some programs, even if the demand for them is economically justifying. Here, for example, one might think of the extended campus doctoral programs that advertise themselves along these lines: "PhDs with one-month residency. Total time including dissertation:

lines: "PhDs with one-month residency. Total time including dissertation:
One Year. Doctorates in 100 fields...."[2] Not so different, perhaps, are some off-campus programs in our urban centers offering MBAs and MPAs to full-time business and public employees, or some degree programs offering credit for life experience, when these programs are justified on the basis of being "money makers for the home campus".

---

[2]From an advertisement in The Chronicale of Higher Education, April 22nd, 1977, Page 21.

9. Will the Plan Stimulate Personal Effort?

As with many, if not all, of these criteria, this is a matter of judgment. The point is: Will the plan serve as a stimulant to good minds, resulting in productive performance that satisfies? For example, it is seldom enough simply to survive, to continue, to maintain. It is better to attempt something that makes the institution unique, or at least relatively distinctive. Generally, the bolder the choice of goals and the wider the range of educational needs served, the more likely the plan is to appeal to the vigorous members of the faculty and administration—yes, and to financial supporters and students as well.

The ambitious upgrading during the 1960s by the University of Massachusetts, Florida State University, and the New York State system meant that their faculties led more stressful professional lives, as might be surmised by examining studies of faculty members in conflict such as those of Bennis, 1973, and Cope, 1972, and the more comprehensive study of the academic profession by Talcott Parsons and Gerald Platt. But the upgrading also provided a stimulating environment for personal achievement. Likewise, the new college experiments along quite different lines at Oakland University, Montieth College, and Evergreen State College appealed to the vigorous nature of other selected faculties and administrations.

10. Is the Strategy Something That Has Been Tried Somewhere Else Where It Was Successful?

Antioch appears to have led the way, demonstrating the viability of world-wide, almost autonomous off-campus programs. Minneapolis's Metropolitan College served as a viable example for upper-division institutions in urban settings. The St. Louis Community College District demonstrated the feasibility of the multi-campus, urban-community-college concept. Yet the PhB, Black Mountain, Monteith, and the Open Admission Program at CCNY are now noble examples in the literature.

While I recommend looking for successful precedents in other similar colleges in similar settings, I emphasize again that each college is unique and each institution will have to "put it all together", each in its own inimitable way.

Summary

Conceiving a strategy that will give the institution an enduring concept of itself, harmonizing its diversity of activities while providing a good fit between opportunities in the environment and institutional strengths, is an extremely-complicated task; so these simple questions—these tests of goodness—will not provide a fail-safe analysis. They will, however, give those concerned with either the formulation of policy or the analysis of alternative policies a good deal to think about as they develop a strategic plan, which as a work of art requires imagination, intuition, and judgment above all else. The following scaled criteria may help those so disposed to quantify the judgmental process. I offer the suggestion that these criteria can be quantified with trepidation.

EVALUATIVE STANDARDS

	Standard	Low	Scale	High
1.	Clarity of Strategy: has Operational Substance.	Ambiguous, Unclear	0 — 5 — 10	Unambiguous, Operational Substance
2.	Strategy Builds Upon Institutional Strengths.	Little Evidence	0 — 5 — 10	Clearly Builds on Strength
3.	Strategy Builds Upon Opportunities in Environment	Seems Unrelated	0 — 5 — 10	Yes, at Least Several Opportunities
4.	Strategy Considers Expectations of Constituencies	Not Considered	0 — 5 — 10	Every Constituent Recognized
5.	Sufficient Resources (Human, Fiscal, Physical) are Available.	Few if any Resources are Available	0 — 5 — 10	Sufficient Resources are Present for Long-Term Needs
6.	Strategy has Internal Consistency.	No Compatibility; Inconsistent	0 — 5 — 10	Much Linked Programming; Focused
7.	Strategy is Compatible with the Aspirations of Staff.	Staff Resistence Would be Substantial	0 — 5 — 10	Clearly in Accord with Aspirations
8.	Strategy is Consistent with Ethical Values, is Socially Responsible.	Questionable Ethical Practice	0 — 5 — 10	Clearly Socially and Ethically Responsible
9.	Strategy is Sufficiently Stimulating to Personal Effort.	Little Challenge	0 — 5 — 10	Challenging
10.	This Strategy has been Successful Somewhere.	No Examples	0 — 5 — 10	Several Successful Applications

Chapter 6

There comes a time in the affairs of men when you must take the bull by the tail and face the situation.

—W.C. Fields

That there is a relationship between clarity of purpose and vigorous educational leadership, on one hand, and institutional vitality and excellence of achievement, on the other, can hardly be doubted.

—Algo Henderson, 1960

THE PRESIDENT AS ARCHITECT OF STRATEGY

Probably one of the most important inaugural address ever given in the United States was presented in 1869 by President Eliot. He had a vision. He knew what he wanted, and drew in detail a specific plan to build a great university out of Harvard College. He retired forty years later, his plan and his vision fulfilled. Gilman of Johns Hopkins likewise knew exactly what Johns Hopkins should be: a graduate research school built on the German model. Tappan, although it cost him his job, knew Michigan's future was in research. Morgan and Dixon of Antioch had visions and saw them fulfilled. It is fair to say that every distinctive college and university owes much of its basic form to presidents with ideas.

These are only a few who stand out among many who have left their remarkable imprint. There are many others, of course: Hannah of Michigan State, Nott of Union, Jordan of Stanford, Harper and Hutchins of Chicago, Brewster of Yale, Suzzallo and Odegaard of Washington, Folwell of Minnesota, Butler of Columbia, Wheeler of California, Birenbaum of the Staten Island Community College, Cosand of the St. Louis Community College District, and many more.

Kerr of California saw the multiple roles of the college president as leader educator, creator, inheritor, wielder of power, and pump, but also as officeholder, caretaker, consensus-seeker, persuader, and bottleneck. Consistent with Kerr's industrial-relations background, he saw the president's chief role as that of mediator. Kerr emphasized his role as mediator as one in which he was largely content to hold the constituencies loosely together while trying to move the whole enterprise ahead inches at a time—essentially a reactive posture, and probably the only feasible posture for the head of that nine-campus system. I would advance two earlier views as better guidance for the president, consistent of course with the concept of strategic planning. About forty years ago (1938) A. Lawrence Lowell stressed the role of the college president as one who retained the initiative for drafting institutional planning, and more "recently" (1953) Chancellor Capen of the University of Buffalo stressed the role of the president as planner, initiator, and co-ordinator. According to Capen, the preoccupation of the president must be on the creation of a "grand plan", or there was no need for a president. I maintain—borrowing a metaphor from the business-policy approach of the Harvard Graduate School of Business—that college presidents should see themselves as "architects of strategy" designing the "grand plan".

As an "architect of strategy" the president takes the lead in searching out and analyzing strategic alternatives, not alone but in concert with the administrative team, the faculty, the trustees, and the other constituencies. As a strategist, the president must above all be an analyst who must choose between alternative designs.

As an architect the president must make strategic choices, so the resulting design is one uniquely adapted to the strengths of the institution, considering the external opportunities and constraints. Hence the president must be imaginative. In addition, since strategy formulation suggests some risk taking, the president will sometimes require the strength to deviate from prevailing designs. Therefore the president must be an innovator who must be prepared to promote and defend those very deviations.

Other metaphors consistent with "architect" and the active, entrepreneural role suggested here include the characterization of the president as conceptualist, statesman, and catalyst: conceptualist to perceive the workable strategy; statesmen to advance and defend it; and catalyst recognizing that as the head of an organization holding little real power, the president acts as an agent of change, carefully channeling staff members' desires for esteem, for status, and for self-actualization into directions consistent with the good of the institution.

The president should seek a simple metaphor to propel the idea of what the institution is or can be. The State University of New York at Buffalo was to become the "Berkeley of the East", the University of Washington the "University of a Thousand Years". Antioch's nature is captured by the "community democracy" metaphor. The University of Southern California is seen as the Avis of the West and the Royal Melbourne Institute of Technology as the MIT of Australia. The University of Michigan employs the imagery associated with the Vital Margin, while little Berea retains the spirit of Great Commitments. Many colleges and universities become "city colleges", junior colleges become "community colleges", and so on. As Bennis points out: "Metaphors have a tremendous power to establish new social realities and to give life and meaning to what was formerly perceived only dimly and imprecisely."

It would seem obvious that the president must be the chief planner, but there are those who have argued for the trustees, state co-ordinating boards, and, most often, the faculty. Still others will recommend important planning responsibilities for a second group: the alumni, legislature, governor, donors, and even accrediting associations. The second group in particular are not in a position to do very much to establish long-term direction. Alumni know the institution as it was; governors and legislatures are voted in and out; donors represent narrow interests; accrediting associations have spasmodic interactions with institutions. No doubt all of these groups have an influence on the directions chosen, but I maintain that their influence has been and properly should remain negligible.

What about the trustees? While boards of trustees have virtually complete and final control over the activities of the institution, they are made up of public-spirited laymen, and quite properly rely on the administration and faculty to develop policies and guidelines. Their role is in restraining direction rather than determining. If they do not like where the institution is being taken by a president, they can replace the president.

State co-ordinating boards have a proper "watchdog" role to play in urging institutions to limit duplication and in restraining unnecessary competition, as well as the role of advisors to the legislature and governor's office on a variety of statewide policies; but they can do little to plan for individual institutions. Any respectable college or university, in fact, ought to treat incursions by state superboards the same way it would treat incursions by the legislature, the governor, donors, or the like—and that is to vigorously defend its integrity.

The faculty participates in important institutional decisions in all but the most autocratic and least sophisticated institutions. Recent years have seen the growing presence of unions guaranteeing the role and process of faculty involvement in decisions, and properly so; but whether unionized or not highly-trained faculty members, as professional specialists with common interests, are organized into discrete schools and departments where their allegiances are already divided between college, department, and field. Of course they as individuals, serving on college or university-wide committees, do contribute genuinely to the enterprise as a whole; but the president and the administration have the main responsibility to represent the interests of all these groups as they assume their inescapable role of viewing the institution as a whole and planning for its total interest.

Practical advantages accrue to a president who develops a clear sense of purpose and clarifies it effectively. First, purpose attracts commitment. The most durable of human motivations is tapped—the aspiration to lend one's strength to causes worth serving.

A second, "mundane", advantage will be that physical-plant development will be shaped by the specifics of the strategic plan's cornerstones. If the base of operations will continue to be the main campus (say) emphasizing a general-education core based (say) upon the humanities, that will mean quite different buildings, offices, seminar facilities, and library accommodations than a plan emphasizing early specialization in scientific and technical subjects with (say) work experiences (internships) in local industrial laboratories.

A third practical advantage is that of a defense against committing resources to a project that captures the "enthusiasm of the moment". A well-considered plan also inspires confidence among funding agencies and donors.

Finally, a strategic plan, openly arrived at, tested, and consistent with enduring values, will be the best defense against the loss of wit and nerve often seen when key personnel leave their posts or when random bits of fiscal grapeshot sweep the air.

Leaders know there is on no campus a monument or a building honoring a committee.

...the potential future for higher education in American society is very great. Whether it proves actually to be so depends on people like us in very specific ways. It depends on whether we have as good a grasp of the larger context of planning as we have of the here-and-now planning process itself. It depends on whether we demonstrate political and educational leadership in higher education that has imagination, daring, and initiative.

—Franklin Patterson, 1977

(*Recommended for the one-foot-long planners' bookshelf)

Ackoff, Russell L., "The Nature and Context of Planning", A Concept of Corporate Planning, Wiley-Interscience, 1970, 1-22.

Adams, Carl R., Theodore Kellogg, and Roger G. Schroeder, "Decision-making and Information Systems in Colleges, Journal of Higher Education, January-February 1976, 33-49.

Anderson, R. E., Strategic Policy Changes at Private Colleges, Teachers' College Press, 1977.

Ansoff, H. I., R. P. Declerck, and R. L. Hayes (editors) From Strategic Planning to Strategic Management, John Wiley and Sons, 1976.

*Balderston, F. E., Managing Today's University, Jossey-Bass, 1974.

*Bergquist, William, and William Shoemaker, "Facilitating Comprehensive Institutional Development", A Comprehensive Approach to Institutional Development, Jossey-Bass, 1976, 1-50.

Boulding, Kenneth E., "The Management of Decline", AGB Reports, September-October 1975, 4-9.

Bowen, Howard, and John Minter, Private Higher Education, Association of American Colleges, 1975.

Capen, Samuel, The Management of Universities, Foster and Steward Publishing Company, Buffalo, 1953.

Christensen, E. P., et al., Business Policy: Text and Cases, Irwin, 1965, and later editions.

Cohen, Michael D., and James G. March, Leadership and Ambiguity: The American College President, McGraw-Hill, 1974.

Conrad, Clifton, "University Goals: An Operative Approach", Journal of Higher Education, October 1974, 504-516.

Cope, Robert, "Economic Variables and the Prediction of College Attendance and Achievement", College and University, 41:1, Fall 1966, 35-40.

Cope, Robert, "Simulation Models Should Replace Formulas for State Budget Requests", College and University Business, 46:3, March 1969, 30-34.

Cope, Robert, "Bases of Power, Administrative Preferences, and Job Satisfaction: A Situational Approach", Journal of Vocational Behavior, 2:4, October 1972, 457-465.

Cope, Robert, "The Effect of Diverse College Environments on American Social Class Structure", Higher Education, 2:2, May 1973, 259-264.

Cope, Robert (editor), Tomorrow's Imperatives Today, Association for Institutional Research, 1973.

Cope, Robert (editor), Public Policy: Issues and Analysis, Association for Institutional Research, 1974.

Cope, Robert (editor), Information for Decisions, Association for Institutional Research, 1975.

Cope, Robert, and William Hannah, Revolving College Doors: The Causes and Consequences of Dropping Out, Stopping Out, and Transferring, John Wiley and Sons, 1975.

Correa, Hector (editor), Analytical Models in Educational Planning and Administration, New York: David McKay Company, Inc., 1975.

Dressel, Paul, and associates, Institutional Research in the University: A Handbook, San Francisco: Jossey-Bass, Inc., 1971.

Enarson, Harold L., "The Art of Planning", Educational Record, Summer 1975, 170-174.

Escher, Firmin, "College of St. Benedict: A Planning Model That Works", in Bergquist, W., and W. Shoemaker, A Comprehensive Approach to Institutional Development, Jossey-Bass, 1976, 51-58.

Escher, Firmin, Directions for the Future, College of St. Benedict, St. Joseph, Minnesota, September 1976.

Fincher, Cameron, "Grand Strategy and the Failure of Consensus", Education Record, Winter 1975, 10-20.

Five College Cooperation: Directions for the Future, Amherst, Massachusetts: University of Massachusetts Press, 1969.

Folk, M., "Computers and Educational Futures Research", in Marien Michael and Warren Ziegler (editors), The Potential of Educational Futures, Charles Jones Publishing Company, Worthington, Ohio, 1972.

Fuller, Bruce, "A Framework for Academic Planning", Journal of Higher Education, 47, January 1976, 65-77.

Glenny, Lyman, "Co-ordination and Planning Despite Competition and Confusion", Allan M. Carter (editor), Assuring Academic Progress Without Growth, New Directions for Institutional Research, Number 6, Summer 1975.

Gregory, A. S., "Strategic Planning of Research and Development at Weyerhaeuser.", Forest Products Journal, 24:9, September 1974, 37-43.

Gubasta, Joseph L., and Norman L. Kaufman, "Developing Information for Academic Management", Journal of Higher Education, 48, July-August 1977, 401-411.

Hambrick, Donald C., and Charles C. Snow, "A Contextual Model of Strategic Decision Making in Organizations" (Mimeo), Pennsylvania State University, June 30th, 1976.

Harvey, L. James, Managing College and Universities by Objectives, Ireland Educational Corporation, 1976.

Harvey, T., "Potential Futures and Institutional Research", Journal of Higher Education, 45:7, October 1974, 517-523.

Henderson, Algo D., The Innovative Spirit, Jossey-Bass, 1970.

Hopkins, David S. P., and William F. Massy, "Long-Range Budget Planning in Private Colleges and Universities", David S. P. Hopkins and Rogert G. Schroeder (editors), Applying Analytic Methods to Planning and Management, New Directions for Institutional Research, Number 13 (Spring 1977).

Jones, Larry R., "Praxis and Context of University and College Academic Planning", Doctoral Dissertation, Berkeley, 1977.

Kibbee, Robert J., "The Hazards of Planning—Predicting Public Policy", in Cope, Robert (editor), Tomorrows's Imperatives Today, Association for Institutional Research, 1973, 23-26.

Knorr, Owen A. (editor), Long-Range Planning in Higher Education, WICHE, Boulder, Colorado, April, 1965.

Ladd, Dwight R., Change in Educational Policy, New York: McGraw-Hill, 1970.

Leister, Douglas V., "Identifying Institutional Clientele", Journal of Higher Education, July-August 1975, 381-398.

Lowell, A. Lawrence, What a University President Has Learned, McMillan, 1938.

Majone, Giandomenico, "The Feasibility of Social Sciences", Policy Sciences, 6, 1975, 49-69.

McGrath, Earl J. (editor), Co-operative Long-Range Planning in Liberal Arts Colleges, New York: Teachers' College, Columbia University, 1964.

*NACUBO, A College Planning Cycle, People, Resources, Process: A Practical Guide, Washington DC: National Association of College and University Business Officers, 1975.

Orton, Don A., and C. Brooklyn Derr, "Crisis and Contingencies for the Small Private College", Teachers' College Record, 77: 2, December 1975, 231-245.

Osborn, A. F., Applied Imagination, Charles Scribner, 1953.

Parekh, Satish B., Long-Range Planning: An Institution-Wide Approach to Increasing Academic Vitality, New Rochelle: Change Magazine, NBW Tower, 10801.

Pardon, Robert, "The Delphi Technique Modified for Establishing Institutional Priorities as a Prerequisite to Resource Allocation", in Clifford Stewart (editor), Reformation and Re-allocation in Higher Education, Association for Institutional Research, 1972, 106-108.

Pardon, Robert, "Delphi Revisited", in Cope, Robert (editor), Information for Decisions, Association for Institutional Research, 1975, 341-343.

Patterson, Franklin, and Charles R. Longsworth, The Making of a College, Cambridge, Massachusetts: MIT Press, 1967.

Patterson, Franklin, "Institutional Planning in the Context of Change", Planning for Higher Education, August 1977, 6, 1-8.

Peterson, Marvin W., "Institutional Research and Policy Formulation: A Contingency Model", in C. Stewart (editor), Institutional Research and Institutional Policy Formulation, Association for Institutional Research, 1971, 27-31.

Pinnell, Charles, et al., Guidelines for Planning and Development in Colleges and Universities, Texas A and M University, College Station, Texas, July 1968 (five volumes).

Prince, G. M., "Creative Meetings Through Power Sharing", Harvard Business Review, July-August 1972, 47-54.

Richardson, Richard C., et al., "The Need for Institutional Planning", Research Currents, ERIC/AAHE, September 1977.

*Richman, Barry M., and Richard N. Farmer, Leadership, Goals, and Power in Higher Education, Jossey-Bass, 1974.

Rourke, Francis, and Glenn Brooks, The Managerial Revolution in Higher Education, Johns Hopkins Press, 1966.

Schroeder, Robert G., Management Information Systems for Colleges and Universities, Working Paper Series, Management Information Systems Research Center, University of Minnesota, August 1975.

Shoemaker, William, "Data and Its Use: A Process System for Planning" (mimeo), Council for the Advancement of Small Colleges, California 1977.

Trivett, David, "The Heuristic Potential of Modern Marketing Theory for Higher Education", a paper prepared for delivery to the Association for the Study of Higher Education, Chicago, March 1978.

Vaccaro, Louis C., "Planning in Higher Education: Approaches and Problems", College and University, 51 (Winter 1976), 153-160.

Whitfield, P. R., Creativity in Industry, Penguin Books, 1975.

Williams, Harry, Planning for Effective Resource Allocation in Universities. Washington: ACE, 1966.